POETRY IN
MOTION PICTURES

By Michael Wood

To Denise
You are a star,
You really are!
Best Wishes
M J Wood

First published in the United Kingdom 2011

Printed and bound in England by Jadan Press Ltd, Unit 27 Argyle Factory Estate, Wyndham Street, Hull, HU3 1HD

Cover design by Nick Matson

The author can be contacted at: iringmybell@yahoo.co.uk

For more on the author visit: www.iringmybell.com

ISBN: 978-0-9568252-0-9

Dedication

For Margaret and Alfie
and
Steven Spielberg.
(Not that Steven Spielberg knows me or is aware
of my work but, hey, it can't harm can it?)

"19th century Britain: I can't stand the style of those times. All those horrible moustaches and breeches and frock coats. It's not very cinematic. I want to make a movie about contemporary America and scare the crap out of the audience." Steven Spielberg on why he switched the action from Victorian England to 21st century New Jersey for the movie *War Of The Worlds*. A comment that doesn't bode well for this author's image, but, as screenwriter William Goldman so famously said about Hollywood: *"Nobody knows anything."*

General Acknowledgements:

Phil Haskins of PFH Productions, who understood the plot from the start and helped to keep it on track. David Alexander and Mark Buck for their wealth of cinema knowledge. Alistair Chisholm, Terry Stubbings and Steve Dale, who also know more about the movies than they realized. Tony Wing and Darren Holmes of The Purple Cow café in Cottingham, who supplied motivational cake, coffee and cosy cinema chat. Jane Halliwell for prompting me to stop staring out of Atkinson's café windows in Willerby and get something published. Ettore Luciano of Luciano's restaurant in Hessle, who will never convince me that De Niro beats Pacino. Sue Lozynskyj and John Fewings of the Subtle Flame poetry group in Beverley, Yorkshire. The Cinema Theatre Association and Harry Rigby the editor of its bi-monthly bulletin. Finally, more than anyone, my thanks to Noel Hudson for never wavering in his belief that I may be on to something and who will now be asking me to introduce him to Jennifer Aniston should Hollywood's studios call. But that'll be after I have firstly wangled an introduction with Angelina Jolie for myself.

Picture Acknowledgements:

Pictures are from the author's collection except:
Lanternist – The Bill Douglas Centre for the History of Cinema and Popular Culture
Eadweard Muybridge – Kingston Museum Heritage Service
Kinetoscope – National Museum of Science and Industry
Tom Mix and Laurel and Hardy – Hull Daily Mail
Johnny Depp – Daryl Green
The National Picture Theatre – Christopher Ketchell
Sir Tom Courtenay – The University of Hull
Julie Christie – Kobal Collection

CONTENTS

THE BUILDING BLOCKS OF CINEMATIC LOVE

It's a given that your gender is female. As such your architectural frontage is akin to a designer ball gown, your ornate marble stairs are stylish shoes, your neon-lit name is the crowning glory of a striking hairdo and you're accessorised by movie posters.

Feasting our eyes on your bodily interior, we are welcomed into the bosom of your plump, velour-crush seats that envelop and hug us. The lights are turned low and the small talk of advertisements then commence. This leads on to the foreplay of movie trailers and, excitingly, it all builds up to the climax of the main feature. The seduction is complete.

For those less smitten you are a casual one night stand, but for those who have fallen under your magic spell, hook, line and cinemascope, you are a life-long love affair.

PROLOGUE

Oyez! Oyez! Oyez! From Old French, sometimes written O yes, its meaning is Hearken! A call made by a town crier, court officer, public announcer etc., to attract attention when a proclamation is about to be read.

O yes! O yes! O yes! A line of racy dialogue cried by Meg Ryan to attract Billy Crystal's attention in the movie When Harry Met Sally.

Between 1887 and 1910 the main traffic artery running through Hollywood was a dirt road called Prospect Avenue. When Hollywood lost its independence and became annexed to Los Angeles (LA), Prospect Avenue was renamed Hollywood Boulevard. I don't believe it would be remiss to change it again to The Make. Why? Because at some time or other everyone in LA has been on it – including me! But when it comes to choosing names, what do I know? Whilst walking the streets of Hollywood it wasn't exactly career enhancing to describe myself as a Public Renaissance Orator (a PRO). Another alternative, a Poet In Motion Pictures (a PIMP), didn't sound too clever either. Whilst Tinseltown Crier had a nice sound to it, on landing the job of helping to promote the area in a positive way, the Hollywood Business Improvement District (my employers) preferred the official title of Hollywood Town Crier.

This situation came about during a break on a town crying assignment to LA in 1999. That's when I took time out to visit the one and only Hollywood! What a disappointment it was. On this first visit I was genuinely shocked at how run-down and dull the central tourist area of Hollywood seemed to be. Nothing was in place to satisfy a visitor's curiosity about its history and heritage in the form of a guided tour along its famous streets. Sure, they had visits to the stars' homes in Beverley Hills but I wanted to know about right here in Hollywood. It motivated me to stick out my brass neck along with my brass bell. Donning my Town Crier's garb I busked my trade along Hollywood Boulevard. To my surprise I was, as they say, talent spotted. One of the city's regeneration big-shots (who also owned the Hollywood Wax Museum) was impressed with my moxie. He asked me to shed light on what he termed "my curious act." In answer I did what everyone else there seems to be so adept at doing, I bigged it up. I explained that I was an internationally known 'meeter and greeter' and, seizing the moment, I pitched the possibility of becoming the city's first ever Town Crier. He showed an interest. A couple of meetings and auditions later I got the gig.

It was concluded that my presence could add a touch of gentrification to Hollywood, which was preparing for a multi-million dollar face lift. I was amazed and elated when offered this appointment. A study of books and documentaries on Hollywood quickly followed. Subsequently my knowledge and respect for the movie business grew, as did a passion for a once great city that was trying to make a comeback as a must-see place on the tourist map.

Originally employed as primary communicators, Town Criers now mostly act as ceremonial announcers and urban cheerleaders for the towns and cities they represent. As such, looking like an extra from *The Madness Of King George*, and not a little un-mad myself, I strolled along Hollywood Boulevard in three layers of clothing under a searing hot sun. My remit was to welcome the 9-million visitors that annually passed through the city and make them feel as though they had arrived. Key to my appointment was pointing out the best places for visitors to spot a star or where they could go and be star-spotted themselves as the next big thing!

The role of a Town Crier through the centuries has been threefold:

- Historically, we communicated news to the illiterate. Thus I was disappointed that my offer to be Arnold Schwarzenegger's voice coach was not taken up.

- Traditionally, we proclaimed the King's proclamations. Thus be it known that Elvis Presley has not only left the building he has also left this earth – definitely and forever!

- Generally, we are very thick skinned. Thus, it's with good grace that we accept all inane comments aimed our way.

Superman and Batman are recognised American superheroes. My look of a renaissance fop is as far removed as possible from the aforementioned – but at least I don't sport a rubber suit like Batman or wear my underpants on the outside like Superman! Ambling along the Walk Of Fame my historic garb elicited many comments that included: "Now there's someone who must have got dressed in a power cut." My stock reply being: "But didn't you know it's all the rage back in England."

Town Criers are often seen as having a piratical look and a frequently heard remark was: "So where is your parrot?" Another stock answer from me being: "She's at home cooking my dinner."

I carried a scroll, which had my title emblazoned across it and I was sometimes asked: "So just exactly who or what is a Town Crier?" My quick reply before giving a proper explanation was: "In Hollywood, I guess it's somebody who has never won an Oscar!"

This two-way good-natured banter was always welcome and brought smiles all around. But the remark that really made me chuckle out loud – that I thought to be a bit rich when coming from LA types – was: "Hey Captain, I was going to ask where your ship is... or should that be space ship?"

On the subject of space, estimates reckon one in ten Americans believe they have experienced abduction by aliens from somewhere in a far off galaxy. But just exactly who's been abducted, where and when did this all happen, are these people for real, or are they what many would call crankcases? From what I saw of life in Hollywood, I believe they all ended up there as extras in what could be renamed Extraterrestrialville. If you want to meet attention-seeking characters – the kind you would normally see cast in a Star Trek movie – then visit Hollywood Boulevard. Believe me, it's the Mecca of the spaced-out where you will experience life, but not as we know it.

When chasing the elusive dream of movie star fame and fortune, it is only ever a lucky few who succeed whilst the majority end up chasing rainbows. For the ones who do make it, somewhere over the rainbow way up high (usually on a billboard), their godlike names appear. This allows mere mortals, of which I am one, to stand below and salute them. That said, those whose celebrity we revere are no more deserving than the people who pay their wages, i.e. the public. I am all for an egalitarian world. However, I realise that Cinema is an escape allowing us to vicariously live our lives through the casting of the bold and the beautiful, not the insignificant or unadorned. Hollywood gives us virtual reality and not the virtue of reality... it's called entertainment.

For those not satisfied at just being a moviegoer but harbour the dream of being one of the adorned and adored movie elite, you may not realise how we actually already contribute to the movies! I offer the following thought on how this contribution goes unrecognised and un-credited, but, most importantly, how it goes unpaid!

STEALING THE SHOW

They steal the chance

to steal into films

where they steal the best lines

whilst stealing the scene

that will ultimately steal our hearts.

Concealed in the dark

we lovingly stare

and then on leaving the cinema

we steal their language

and we steal their look

but yet we're only taking back

what they stole from us!

During my first time in Hollywood, an irony not lost on me and all other visitors was that as a business it could create a chocolate-box-covered-look as the background for a film and proudly show it on the big screen – yet as a place it had failed. However, 700 million dollars of public money and 5 billion dollars of private funds would be invested for improvements between 2000 and 2010. Hollywood was making a comeback, which had given me the opportunity to bring my entertainment and people skills to use.

Normally a Town Crier would have a bell as an attention-seeking tool. I furnished myself with not only a bell, but also a crumhorn and a small car hooter, the latter instrument being the type used by Harpo of the Marx Brothers. For my meet and greet act, I felt that I needed to have the equivalent of a catchphrase. As such, I theatrically regaled a welcoming ditty to amused tourists:

OYEZ! OYEZ! OYEZ!

Visitor, resident, pauper, President?

Don't be shy as you walk by,

Hear my cry, whereby,

I honk my hooter, I ring my bell,

I sound my horn and I loudly yell,

WELCOME TO HOLLYWOOD!

What more can I say, but this final hooray,

God bless America, God save *my* Queen,

And you have a nice day!

The recording button of tourists and visiting film crews' cameras are always on in the carnival atmosphere of Hollywood, and my job was to play to them. My welcome went down well, with repeat requests to mention a person or a family name placed before the "have a nice day" line.

In an attempt to vary my act, a tune I remembered from being a young lad was one from the opening credits of the classic British television programme Robin Hood starring Richard Greene (you can see it on YouTube). I have always fancied myself as a bit of singer and, though nobody else has, it has never stopped me! In the style of an old Hollywood tenor of the fifties, with all the histrionics I could muster, I performed to tourists my own words to the Robin Hood theme tune:

♫ I'm Michael Wood, Michael Wood, on the Boulevard,

In Hollywood, Hollywood, as a rhyming bard,

When I deliver my stanza,

I sing it like Mario Lanza,

What could be worse...

than listening to...

poetic verse? ♫

(I bet you're singing this right now, aren't you?) Often asked if I said poetic or pathetic, my offering to the world of opera occasioned smiles from a bemused public, though I suspect more in sympathy than in support.

"Whoever writes your material I would sue," someone told me. With resignation I replied: "I did and I lost, that's why I do what I do!"

It was suggested to me by a local resident that because most Americans were not familiar with the Robin Hood television program I should try adapting some words to fit the theme tune of America's one time favourite cowboy serial, the Lone Ranger. (The Lone Ranger music is, of course, taken from the William Tell Overture by composer Gioachino Rossiniand and is a dramatically fast moving piece of music.) I was pleased that my presence was being warmed to and I initially rose to this challenge, but then I dropped the idea for I didn't want to turn what might be seen as eccentricity into parody.

I loved every minute of my time working in Hollywood. Thankfully I was a hit with the media for I gained plenty of newspaper copy and I appeared in several LA television entertainment features. My positive experiences motivated me to write a more serious ode celebrating what is for some the entertainment capital of the world, but for me is the world's most fickle place the majority of us know fickle all about.

I CRIED AND HOLLYWOOD LAUGHED

Should you be seeking an eighth deadly sin?
Look to Hollywood, it's all there within,
It's failure and despair, it's fab and big bucks,
It's classy and awesome, it's sleazy, it sucks!

It's where swords will never be mightier than pens,
It's where one hopes to be the light through the lens,
It's where you'll succeed by the art of glad handing,
And where kneeling puts you in the right standing!

It's where ordinary folk found riches and fame,
Monroe, Pacino, Travolta, John Wayne,
It's where Bruno and Borat, each a crass clown,
Boldly succeeded when they came on down.

It's where you should visit for it could be you there,
Who's just been spotted by a famous producer,
Because in Hollywood you will see,
Anything goes – look what happened to me!

Since the birth of cinema, lodged in between the two genre bookends of comedy and tragedy, there are countless visual and vocal iconic moments which could be described as poetry – indeed, poetry in motion pictures.

What can surpass Laurel and Hardy delivering a piano; a soliloquy from Orson Welles on the merits of cuckoo clocks; Fred Astaire putting on the Ritz; Bacall asking Bogart if he knows how to whistle; Burt Lancaster's laugh; John Wayne's walk; Ursula Andress emerging from the surf in *Dr No;* Will Smith welcoming aliens to earth; Clint Eastwood asking punks to get off his lawn; *Star Trek* still boldly going through split infinitives; and although Tom Cruise's bank balance is probably poetic to him it doesn't make this brief list.

Part one of this book, which was inspired by my Hollywood experiences and my love of cinema, is an abridged look at cinema's history, covering some of its memorable moments in the form of verse. Attempting such a task was not without difficulty. The main problem was deciding on what to include whilst avoiding the trap of sinking under the weight of too many references, names and dates. I resolved this in three ways:

Firstly, I simply wrote of what I liked about the movies. Secondly, I included what I had learned when employed as the Hollywood Town Crier. Thirdly, in order to keep a sense of scale I concentrated on American cinema rather than the vast subject of 'world cinema'.

The final problem was choosing a poetic beat and meter that would sustain throughout its epic length. What I settled on could best be described as having a 'rap' feel.

Unlike movie director Jim Cameron, who worked solid for 14 years on *Avatar (2009)*, it was over a lesser amount of years that I had been periodically jotting down notes to turn into verse for this book. I cannot imagine how much Cameron's life is consumed by his passion to create such fantastic film work. My own passion had me at times feeling like the frustrated – though some would say crazed – word processing character played by Martin Short in Scorsese's underrated gem *After Hours* (1985). Why did I undertake such a labour? Because frankly, my dear reader, I do give a damn.

But at what point in time should I conclude what I was composing? Seeing *Avatar* in 3-D helped me to decide. A cinematic milestone equal to the coming of sound, Technicolor and IMAX, Cameron's epic, special-effects blockbuster proved a worthy high point for me to wrap up part one.

During the time spent writing parts two and three of this book, a film about a guy with a speech impediment began doing the rounds. This wasn't Jeff Bridges in *True Grit* (2010); it was Colin Firth in *The King's Speech* (2010). Though I should have had this book at the printers well over a month ago, out of British patriotism I delayed doing so until today, which is the morning after the results of the 2011, 83rd Annual Academy Awards. Movies are about lights, camera, action. *The King's Speech*, a low-budget British produced period drama, is about lights, camera, articulation – yet it took four major Oscars, including the big one for Best Picture. How? Some may say it was made with a deliberate view to ticking all the boxes in the Oscar rule book; the less cynical will say it was simply because of cinematic storytelling at its very best. What I say is that it m m m m more than deserved all of its plaudits!

I'd like to finish this introduction by admitting that I know Darth Vader is two faced, but I am with him in seeking the dark side. As God – or was it Cecil B Demille – once said: "Let there be light," and there was light. As Cinema said: "Let the lights be dimmed," and they were dimmed.

PART ONE

THE HISTORY OF AMERICAN CINEMA (ABRIDGED)

The kind of story than can never bore me
is the one that's told in silver screen glory.

THE LIGHT THROUGH THE LENS

"Hell, there are no rules – we're trying to accomplish something."
Thomas A. Edison

The combination for the creation
to make a Magic Lantern occasion,
Are the basic gems of brushes and pens,
paint pots, glass plates, oil lamp and lens,
For years umpteen these items have seen
imagery projected on to a screen,
For peasants or kings, in tents or inns,
travelling lanternists rattled their tins,
And as coins flowed magic images glowed
which progress eventually overshadowed,
For in due course the material source
from erstwhile inventions took its force.

In the year of 1873,
an American horse ran wild and free,
A photograph made which when surveyed,
couldn't fully prove its hooves were all raised,
Several years on Edward Muybridge was done
and his pictures of motion he'd laboured on,
Proved it for sure, but his plat du jour
was his Zoopraxiscope which helped procure,
A keen affection for film projection
and the race had begun for its perfection,
History then rated that what he'd created
was film's first projector for which he's feted.

In 1884 it oversaw
the moving image develop yet more,

The Kinetoscope pushed the envelope
and was Thomas Edison's breakthrough hope,
Although sublime its only crime
was only one person could view at a time,
His peepshow machine was very soon seen
from New York onwards and this did mean,
Big money signs in neat straight lines
for other inventors and their designs.

In 1895 film did thrive
when in Paris, France, still-life came alive,
Hitting pay day and leading the way
the Lumiere brothers earned cachet,
Their box of tricks knocked us for six
with its camera, printer and projector mix,
On shining a light intense and bright
through their Cinematograph – what a sight!
A vision of awe rarely seen before,
the Cinematograph helped to ensure,
Not having to queue could now ensue
and communal viewing was key to its coup.

Inventions galore became the big draw
whilst entrepreneurs waged a patents war,
Stateside things just grew, grew and grew,
but cutting things short let's move on to,
1909 when deemed a swine
Thomas Edison flicked a V-sign,
For unarguably and demonstrably
he'd cornered cinema's monopoly,
His east coast sway caused a breakaway;
California beckoned, especially L.A.,
Then burning benzene a movement was seen,
as filmmakers journeyed to grass more green.

THE SILENT ERA

"For the love scenes in my first Hollywood silent picture
Dark Angel, I spoke in my own language, Hungarian, and
my co-star, Ronald Colman, chatted about cricket and
kippers."
Vilma Banky

"Once upon a time," what an opening line
for a *true* story about a goldmine,
Called Hollywood where little once stood
on its open expanse of hills and mud,
Where from the seas an ocean breeze
cooled low-raise crops and tall palm trees,
Where the warm sun shone down upon
picturesque homes drawing folks to come,
To afternoon nap in a paradise trap
at a quiet idyll on America's map,
Then Nestor came to earn the fame
of the first studio to stake its claim,
In 1911 when an earthly heaven
was born and matured by 1927.

The magic notion of pictures in motion
charmed the people with its heady potion,
A converted store would open its door
and audiences sat in wondrous awe,
A wooden seat, a large white sheet
and projector to make the show complete,
Showed good and bad, joyous and sad,
flickering images of hero and cad,
Peasant or gentry paid five-cents entry
into Nickelodeons without passementerie,
Then something more grand made a stand
when Picture Palaces abounded the land.

The acting few saw their fame accrue
and a studio-system made its debut,
When the prominence and true provenance
of the first filmstar was Florence Lawrence,
A picture success, more or less,
featured a damsel in dire distress,
When pretty faces found their places
alongside those of rogues or nutcases,
Cue Pearl White's silent screams of fright
as moustached villains cackled with delight,
To further astound and aid lack of sound
a lively piano played in the background,
But a bigger hit was when in the pit
a full on orchestra did their bit.

Silver screen cuties fulfilled their duties
of being fully-clothed bathing beauties,
The not so pure Theda Bara's allure
gave her sex-symbol status for sure,
Exotically swanky Vilma Banky
also gave hint to some hanky panky,
The sultry looks of Louise Brooks
and her bob-haircut made history books,
We couldn't wish for a better dish
than served by ingénue Lillian Gish,
But of all the girls the pick of the pearls
was Mary Pickford and her golden curls.

His leathery face, charisma and pace,
made Douglas Fairbanks a swashbuckling ace,
Will Rogers was cheered, Lon Chaney was jeered,
Tom Mix the cowboy was loved and revered,
John Gilbert hosted looks to be boasted
and Ronald Colman was equally toasted,

No one could pan or not be a fan
of Lionel and John of the Barrymore clan,
Richard Barthelmess made a success
as someone to offer a kiss and caress,
But film's best lover above any other
was Valentino – just ask your mother.

Slapstick's arrival and its survival
was through two famous producing rivals,
With equal merit the two we credit
are witty Hal Roach and droll Mack Sennett,
A custard-pie thrown in the eye
by Mabel Normand showed us all why,
When taking the mick what did the trick
was knockabout slapstick, fast and thick,
Just who could top the old Keystone Cop
or Harold Lloyd with a bucket and mop?
Only the blend of a fat and thin friend,
yes, Laurel and Hardy a true godsend.

Ben Turpin's bumbling, cross-eyed stumbling,
pratfalling clown was charmingly humbling,
And never once hissed, Harry Landon's gist
was that of a childlike pantomimist,
But nought could outshine or ever sideline
the sympathetic tramp played so divine
by Chaplin who became with just acclaim
the planet's most famous silver-screen name,
Though also as good, Keaton has stood
as someone deserving of film sainthood,
his do and dare and stone-faced stare
were genius gifts deserving fanfare.

Films early spell deserves to tell
of Laemmle and Lasky who did excel,

These great producers introduced us
to the art of film that so seduced us,
Earning their due were directors too
and D W Griffith gave me and you,
Many a tale on the grandest scale,
like *Birth Of A Nation* – bewailed and regaled,
Cecil B De Mille also thrilled
with spectacular epics on the bill,
Some may gush at Chaplin's *The Gold Rush*
whilst other folk think it romantic slush,
Of more consequence is *Intolerance*
about love and its bigoted predominance,
Without false pomp a love that stomped
its mark as the era's superior romp
is the venerable and the memorable
Buster Keaton's masterpiece *The General*.

Shyster to scholar, folks chased the dollar,
'lights, camera, action' was the main holler,
from overbearing foul mouthed swearing,
high-boots, breeches and monocle wearing
directors who strove and cleverly drove
their crew to produce a film treasure trove
of genres galore about love or war,
horror, westerns, sci-fi and more.

Under arc-lamps be it kids or tramps,
conquerors or clowns, flappers or vamps,
Be it with pens or behind the lens
we can only give thanks and by the tens,
To the pioneers of those early years
who constantly stretched film-making frontiers,
From cinema's start they played their part
to advance film as a consummate art.

THE HOLLYWOOD YEAR THAT WAS!

*"I've been to Paris France and I've been to Paris Paramount.
Paris Paramount is better."*
Ernst Lubitsch

A 'dream factory' brought you and me
an escape from life's dull drudgery,
The glitz and glamour we did clamour
was there to be seen in Hollywood's manor,
Take 1922 what a hullabaloo,
the Egyptian Theatre saw the debut,
Of limos in flight to arrive by night
as skyward-beaming lights burned bright,
And rushing from bars crowds shouted "hurrahs"
to see red carpets and Tuxedo-clad stars,
When the entrepreneur with creative flair
Sid Grauman began the first film premiere,
And thousands stood to watch *Robin Hood*,
aka Doug Fairbanks who'd shed his blood,
To earn the crown and great renown
of being the first royal of Tinseltown.

Then five years on standing second to none,
in the filmmakers' Mecca the deal was done,
L.A. could boast at being the host
to all major studios – coast to coast,
When most notably, Sid gave you and me
the Chinese Theatre and epitome
of movie house glory and the story
of a tradition of hoary vainglory,
with proud loyalty it's had the novelty
for the hand and footprints of movie royalty.

'27 was sublime and it defined
in Hollywood history a crucial time,
The Academy of Motion Picture, Arts and Sciences
formed against Union alliances,
Al Johnson broke ground when cinema found
the best way of finally including sound,
"You aint heard nothing yet," did beget
worry on every film studio set,
It was all change as directors deranged
sacked all actors who were vocally strange,
Like the once great John Gilbert whose fate
was dying from booze, but he did create,
Something to mourn from which we've drawn
for based on his life came *A Star Is Born.*

The show must go on and not before long
'silents' were history and 'talkies' the one,
When Broadway's best came out west
that saw stage actors breeze the screen test,
So went this epoch when around the clock
as moths to bright light others did flock,
To the Promised Land with suitcase in hand
like the past 'gold rush' but this time the stand,
Was to strike a claim in a movie frame –
get discovered was the name of the game,
Hopefuls, dreamers, romantics, schemers,
some became stars... others waiters or cleaners.

THE CASTING COUCH

"I had to go and see this guy, very important man, and everyone said: 'Watch out Shelly, the second you get into his office he'll tear your dress off'. I'll remember, I said, I'll wear an old dress."
Shelley Winters

High or low key the film matinee
was favoured as the one fun place to be,
This welcome digression helped to lessen
troubled dark days of the The Great Depression,
Eight studios in all stood proud and tall
and come the '30's enthralling us all,
Nurturing narcissists had on the list
Columbia, Universal and United Artists,
But cream of the crop saw MGM top
with Paramount, Warner Bros, RKO and Fox.

Airily above us and hardnosed to others
did studio chiefs' fathers marry their mothers?
A question fair, for studio chiefs were
ruthless when trying to beat their confrere,
Like big picture player Louis B. Mayer,
Zukor, Thalberg or Goldwyn the soothsayer,
From wheeler-dealers trying to steal us
to come and view their one and two reelers,
To moguls yielding and tightly shielding
the power and glory they were wielding,
Film moguls hail thee with destiny
over a please-choose-me star wannabe,
When the pain of hiring or joy of firing
were not as much fun as doing the siring,
Cue Harry Cohn the meanest man known;
it's said the casting-couch was his throne,

So it did go in the business called 'show',
just ask the blonde-bombshell Jean Harlow,
She knew all the moves like Howard Hughes,
a Hollywood-flier who gave starlets cues,
It wasn't that actors had no detractors
as scandals exposed them as malefactors,
Take Clara Bow who sadly did go
a shameless route which we wanted to know,
But we did moan that morals be shown
when Fatty Arbuckle's scandal was known,
Against the suborned The Hays Code formed;
a self-regulation for all the adorned,
In Sodom-by-the-Sea that dubiously
Hollywood was called for its infamy.

Picture the scene as a stretch limousine
pulls-up alongside to deliver a dream,
The window winds down, you smile from a frown
as a mover and shaker from Tinseltown,
Tells you that: "If you'd like to act
you could have stardom and that's a fact,"
Although you vouched the casting couch
would never see you on your knees crouched,
Thrown is the dice and you pay the price,
in life's big scheme it's a small sacrifice,
You wine and dine at Hollywood and Vine
where a contract is given for you to sign,
On reaching your goal you're on the payroll
but the studio system now owns your soul,
Yet hey, so what, you've hit the jackpot
soon you'll be working the movie backlot,
When oh the thrill when one might trill:
"I'm ready when you are Mr De Mille,"
And come a new dawn a star could be born
for those sat watching whilst eating popcorn.

THE GOLDEN AGE OF MOVIE STARS

*"Disney, of course, has the best casting. If he doesn't like
an actor he just tears him up."*
Alfred Hitchcock

When sitting front-row we saw love flow
towards our heroine or our hero,
When oh so able, legend and fable,
first King of Hollywood was Clark Gable,
A nature's crime to heaven consigned
his wife Carole Lombard whilst in her prime,
We mourned the day she passed away
but 'the show must go on' rang the cliché,
For careers to last they led certain paths
and for many it helped to be typecast,
A perfect pact, twixt writer and act,
was Shakespeare and Olivier that's a fact,
Whilst gin and tonic made the historic
W.C. Fields the best sour-note comic,
Spencer Tracy and Katherine Hepburn
made the best screwball comic turn,
Whilst Deborah Kerr had a cute derriere
only matched by Cary Grant's savoir-faire.

Lack of fast car or cigar in a bar
helped Shirley Temple become a child star,
The girl next door with song, dance and more
was Debbie Reynolds, whom all did adore,
When Barbara Stanwyck was in a flick
bold and outspoken she never took shtick,
Helping to bridge racial linkage
cue the short lived Dorothy Dandridge,
For females hurt, Claudette Colbert
attested womanhood – that was a cert,

Caustic Mae West was easily the best
at sublime put-downs that have stood time's test,
A cigarette clung whilst words were sung,
that's Marlene Dietrich the femme fatale hun,
What a blast with her chequered past
as a bitch Joan Crawford was perfectly cast.

Her splendour lauded, her talent applauded,
Rita Haworth used what nature afforded,
Like Vivien Leigh who vivaciously
graced screen and stage with looks must-see,
Making heads turn was Audrey Hepburn
the embodiment of a physical nocturne,
Sex goddess Ava how men did crave her,
her figure made music quiver and quaver,
And what could better the sinfonietta
of Lana Turner in a tight fitting sweater,
The feisty gem Sophia Loren
thanked pasta for making her 'ten out of ten',
The sensuous tone of Garbo's groan:
"I want to be alone," warmed testosterone,
The wherewithal of Lauren Bacall
and cool Grace Kelly had men in their thrall,
Her acting was flawed but men adored
Jane Russell's assets that were once outlawed,
Without failure men's genitalia
beat like their hearts for Elizabeth Taylor,
But oh Tallula no one could rule her,
her libido caused much Hallelujah.

A biblical tale could never fail
with Charlton Heston playing lead male,
Flash Errol Flynn always managed to win
the sword-fight or shoot-out that he was in,

The loveable dope trying to cope
was wisecracking chump, vaudevillian Bob Hope,
The Marx Brothers team were simply supreme
at anarchic comedy in the extreme,
The somewhat shy all American pie
Henry Fonda was cinema's nice guy,
Whereas for some like Robert Mitchum
his tough guy persona was much more fun,
One who spent his time content
was David Niven the debonair gent,
Whilst dimpled Kirk and smiling Burt
were action-men making villains eat dirt,
And casting's need for a villain to bleed
saw Basil Rathbone fitting the deed.

Straight to the top a career then flopped
when Orson Welles met a sudden stop,
When Bogart played trench-coated Sam Spade
there was never a role so tailor-made,
Tough James Cagney was also handy
when dancing in *Yankee Doodle Dandy*,
When wrong existed and right resisted
Gregory Peck's service was often enlisted,
Hanging up his gun then into the sun
rode Jimmy Stewart when The West was won,
It's surely no lie that cinema's 'why'
was so that cowboys rode tall as the sky,
And wisest to warmest, largest to smallest,
big John Wayne was the one who rode tallest.

The good and the great then accepted fate
for old-age meant a change of nameplate,
The stars that shone and hearts they won
in the 'golden age' would soon be gone,

Old Hollywood's class were put out to grass
whilst in the wings was a volte-face,
Enter James Dean on to the scene
along with an angel called Norma Jean,
For whom we cried universally wide
when before their time they tragically died,
Their lives were short and we were taught
talent is something not borrowed nor bought,
As we found out from Brando's clout;
the best male contender without a doubt!
when at his peak his strong physique
made others look a mere pipsqueak,
his acting method saw him shepherd
a style in movies that soon was peppered
with imitators and tailgaters
though none could ever match his status.

But Brando aside, from the starry eyed
great female talent, what can't be denied,
Monroe had the sass and Hepburn the class
but the one with these and a neck of brass,
was the unfettered and no way bettered
Bette Davis, to whom we're indebted,
just who could excel her heaven or hell,
good Bette, bad Bette, either was swell,
what could outshine when she spoke a line
like: "What a dump," or "You dirty swine,"
or one of film noirs best au revoirs:
"Why ask for the moon when we have the stars."

THE GOLDEN AGE OF MOVIE MAKING

*"The actors were all in their places – looking at me
expectantly. I'd no idea what was required. Finally my
assistant, the splendid Jack Sullivan, whispered: 'Say
action'. I did and The Maltese Falcon was underway."*
John Huston – on his directing debut

How we'd hurry to join the flurry
of getting good seats and the only worry,
Was genuine fret when searching for Rhett
and equally the drama to find a Scarlett,
When wunderkind and determined
David Selznick made *Gone With The Wind*,
Which history defined through its tagline:
'The most magnificent film of all time'.

Many films shown were just a clone
of over-acting and lacking in backbone,
Show knights in armour not melodrama,
give us flawed heroes or a drunk charmer,
Like *The African Queen* a film to be seen
and a model cinematic evergreen,
For bad against good a classic that's stood
is the fabulous *Adventures Of Robin Hood*,
Westerns we opine, John Ford defined
with the classic *My Darling Clementine*,
His *Stagecoach* too helped to undo
the inertia westerns were then going through,
Nonetheless super was Gary Cooper
in *High Noon* as the stand-alone trooper,
With his small frame Allan Ladd became
'larger than life' in the brilliant *Shane*,
Though not real Mcoys but still a big noise
were Gene and Roy the singing cowboys.

Frank Capra's delight *It Happened One Night*
took five main Oscars – and quite right,
Though trouble and strife can often be rife
Capra also showed *It's A Wonderful Life,*
Thank God we've got *Some Like It Hot*
an ace Billy Wilder comedy plot,
But Alfred Hitchcock how his films shocked
especially a *Psycho* off his block,
We must regale on a similar scale
the horror master director James Whale,
When flipping heck a doctor's check
showed *Frankenstein* impotent (his nuts were in his neck),
And a figure of dark making his mark
was *Dracula* whose bite was worse than his bark,
But how we adored *King Kong* when he roared,
a beast who by beauty was tragically floored,
To great acclaim mobster-movies became
a winning hit in a movie frame,
The then franchise of playing tough guys
saw Edward G. Robinson taking first prize,
Not so contrasting was Bogey's casting
in *Casablanca* – a film everlasting,
and As Times Goes By will film's alumni
allow Ingrid Bergman to fade and die?

Part of cinema's pull and seduction
was the delight of a left-field production,
Like when if because a wizard there was,
it could only have been *The Wizard of Oz,*
Plan 9 From Outer Space took first place
as the worst film made in the human race,
and director Ed Wood has bravely stood
as king of the phrase: "It's so bad its good."

Hearts were alight at Disney's *Snow White;*
the first full-length-animated-film delight,
Then we heard cries at the shock surprise
when *Bambi*'s mum sadly met her demise,
Yet who could fault our Uncle Walt
and the charms in his Magic Kingdom's vault,
He at least had nous to know Mickey Mouse
would always be playing to a full house.

Sequins, crown-toppers and showgirl's whoppers
featured in Busby Berkeley showstoppers,
Who could sing and our hearts win
like Judy Garland, Sinatra and Bing,
Gliding on air what could we compare
to the heavenly steps of Fred Astaire?
Only the serene acrobatic Gene
who soared and spiralled across the big screen,
And *Singing In The Rain* will surely remain
the best ever musical in film's domain.

Religious flicks couldn't be licked
cue the bible as a script always picked,
Or if in doubt a producer's shout
was: "Let's make a western they carry clout,"
The dark perplexity of *Double Indemnity*
is thought as the very first film noir entity,
A film to befriend that didn't pretend
are lesser known gems like *The Lost Weekend,*
A great film choice over which to rejoice
is *All About Eve* with its urbane voice,
Of cultural brilliance and cognizance
Sunset Boulevard portrayed insignificance,
Though time and again critics all claim
the height of filmmaking is *Citizen Kane.*

A time came when a 'list of ten'
were told "you won't work in this town again",
U.S. piety and anxiety
banned Communists from film society,
A fear of Reds in Hollywood beds
polarised talents and poisoned heads,
The House Un-American Activities
put paid to left wing proclivities,
This dark campaign caused hurt and pain,
careers faltered and didn't sustain,
For movies must be patriotically
right wing, pro-American and sex free.

A history page that won't be upstaged
were the '30's and '40's; 'The Golden Age',
The 50's brought shift which saw folks drift
back to their homes and rather swift,
TV came along to sing a new song
signalling a possible denouement,
Of three decades of the best films made
from which the public now slowly swayed,
For cinemas fuller with films less duller
hail Cinemascope and Technicolor,
Sound-systems chronic got the right tonic
when graded up to stereophonic,
And the new grandiose short-term dose
of 3-D should have kept us all engrossed,
Yet naught could forestall written on the wall
was that cinema faced a mighty fall.

THE SIXTIES AND A NEW HOLLYWOOD

*"America may be violent, greedy and colonialist but my God,
it's interesting."*
Paul Newman

We said hooray to TWA
for in '61 they paved the way,
Now during one's trip no need to kip
'cos in-flight-movies made flying hip,
A requisition had also arisen
for movies to be made for Television,
A welcome slew of foreign films too
with arthouse élan made their breakthrough,
Kids, marijuana, kitchen sink dramas
now challenged big epic panoramas,
Bold extremes filled up our screens
of sex and drugs and rock 'n' roll themes,
Twee Sandra Dee and her virginity
was forever consigned to history.

We said cheerio to RKO
and The Studio System was no more,
Film players now they didn't kow-tow
to studio chiefs and their great know-how,
Bold grandstanding saw actors demanding
that contracts be met with understanding,
Film in sprocket meant money in pocket
and the stars' demands began to skyrocket,
Raising the bar, Liz Taylor the star
got a million for *Cleopatra,* ha ha ha!
This movie disaster with no sticking-plaster
bled money and reputations even faster,
Beyond the pale it was the Holy Grail
of the blueprint for how to successfully fail.

Change upon change brought a new range
of faces and names; some known, some strange,
Take Steve McQueen, rugged and lean
and the 'king of cool' both on and off screen,
For swimming-pool-eyes as blue as the skies,
even more handsome Paul Newman applies,
Making his mark, Robert Redford sparked
in the class rom-com *Barefoot In The Park*,
Sean Connery spoke and the world awoke
to "Bond, James Bond," an alpha-male bloke,
Standing 6:4 with required square jaw
Clint Eastwood proved box-office quick-draw.

Forgetting roughnecks with buffed-up pecs
Michael Caine showed it was cool to wear specs,
With natural ease Jack Lemmon could squeeze
a light comic part or shady unease,
Face weatherbeaten and not one to sweeten
Charles Bronson's role was turning the heat on,
Lee Marvin's thanked for the thrilling *Point Blank,*
his vicious demeanour was cash in the bank,
But the best date with an evil portrait?
Jack Palance easily held that mandate!

On agents' books but not just for looks
Natalie Wood's talent earned the bucks,
In the same vein was Shirley MacLaine
whose spiritual stance also entertained,
No need to ponder that beauty Jane Fonda
made men's eyes never want to wander,
So could we say of Faye Dunaway
and fab Ann Margaret who took breath away,
Men will concur they couldn't but stare
at Raquel Welsh in a bikini of fur,

But men will confess the day they bless
was the hot beach-shot of Ursula Andress.

Making girls stare with his ducktail-hair
Tony Curtis embodied laissez faire,
He gave inspiration to one of his nation;
Elvis the bouffanted singing-sensation,
The swivelling hip and the curling lip
suited The Colonel's entrepreneurship,
And for a time during Elvis's prime
his early films had committed no crime,
A script in his palm then lost him his charm
on the day he sang Old McDonald's Farm,
Our hair went grey like The King's heyday
whose fun-filled frolics became passé,
As were the ones with Doris Day songs
her musicals became dated contretemps,
Way deep inside, folks could not abide
the same old song and together they sighed,
Then came rave reviews causing record queues
for *The Sound Of Music* with Julie Andrews,
Which just goes to show what do film fans know
about what to accept and what to forego!

Things felt celibate until *The Graduate*
a bittersweet tale about an inadequate,
A shot in the arm giving censors alarm
was *Bonny And Clyde* with its violent charm,
When eggs made him puke no critic rebuked
everyone's hero *Cool Hand Luke,*
Westerns found favour with a new saviour,
spaghetti not steak was the new flavour,
Forget the umbrella, cue panatela,
bye *Mary Poppins*, hi *Barbarella.*

Equality of race found a birthplace
in a film with a startling slap of a face,
In The Heat Of The Night justly incites
the cause for blacks and their Civil Rights,
With due respect and credit bedecked
Sidney Poitier is therefore name-checked.

Some think its lame the B-movie game
but it earned Roger Corman legendary fame,
Without a debate his peers did rate
his prolific output as justly great,
Hot-wiring filmmaking at speed breathtaking
his foot hit the gas and caused an awakening.

A defiant divorce had taken force;
New Hollywood replaced the old warhorse,
A hit was found in this turnaround
and *Midnight Cowboy* became renowned
as the first X-rated to be celebrated –
its Best Picture Oscar was rightly feted,
But stealing the show of this new credo
was *Easy Rider* which helped minds blow,
A modus operandi riding high
was the movie genre that just wouldn't die,
Westerns did bid to be less pilloried
cue *Butch Cassidy And The Sundance Kid,*
And in the same year came an all-clear
for unchecked violence in films without fear,
It caused a divide how *The Wild Bunch* died
which left movies now without much to hide,
But the sixties signatory soliloquy?
2001: A Space Odyssey.

THE SEVENTIES

*"The title Star Wars was an insurance policy. We calculated
there are something like 8 million worth (sic) of science
fiction freaks in the USA and they will go see absolutely
anything with a title like Star Wars."*
George Lucas

Cinema enhanced the very real chance
of exploiting longed-for back-seat romance,
When ushers did seat-ya for the creature
of the lamented double-film-feature,
But numbers were down and heading to town
to help movie-going regain its crown,
Was the big draw of films by the score
when the multiplex opened a welcome door.

Playing the zero or playing the hero
we hailed Pacino and De Niro,
But put to the test we'd vote Jack best
for *One Flew Over The Cuckoo's Nest,*
When up to bat, Clint had begat
his style was action not indulging in chat,
Woody, however, went hell for leather
as the king of one-liners, quick and clever,
For an artisan with many a fan,
cue Dustin Hoffman the *Little Big Man,*
Gene Hackman too managed to imbue
as an actor there isn't much he can't do,
Sylvester Stallone braved it alone
and *Rocky* became universally known,
Another achiever was musical diva
John Travolta in *Saturday Night Fever,*
Whilst Marlon Brando wouldn't fandango,
instead in Paris he danced the last tango.

Though critics panned it fans still demand it,
the popcorn smash *Smokey And The Bandit,*
Its amiable star and cop's bête noir
was tough Burt Reynolds who drove a fast car,
But one must mention *The French Connection*
for a car chase with the greatest tension,
This film's epithet is that it set
the standard for 'cop film' etiquette.

Another film craft brought us a raft
of blaxploitation movies like *Shaft,*
We got on down with *Foxy Brown*
and soul and funk and jive and motown,
The genre creation of 'exploitation'
pushed the boundaries to thrill the nation,
They had no taste and were in your face
but they sure as hell had a marketplace,
Creepy or cheesy, slasher or sleazy,
such were the themes of films cheap and easy,
Take your seat for the lurid *Caged Heat*
but don't run screaming out into the street
on hearing the cries in *The Hills Have Eyes*
'cos the lucky die first you'll soon realise.

A free for all increased footfall
when zombie violence set out its stall,
Gathering pace, dystopian waste
and post apocalyptic found its place,
Dawn Of The Dead was way ahead
at making us sleep uneasy in bed,
The battering ram of better film flan
was the true classic *The Omega Man,*
We gladly traipsed for opening of drapes
for the first and best *Planet Of The Apes.*

More than half-hearted a genre imparted
a run of films which *Airport* had started,
Disaster films beat most film disasters
and Irwin Allen was one of their masters,
A deathly ergo and destructive concerto
was witnessed in *The Towering Inferno,*
This time using the theme of cruising,
The Poseidon Adventure was also bruising,
But what brainstorm thought it good form
to inflict on the world (without warning) *The Swarm.*

Upon an invite would we delight
in boarding a spaceship on a strange flight
To heaven knows where on merely a prayer;
have we the courage and have we the dare?
This question you'll find comes to one's mind
for *Close Encounters Of The Third Kind,*
But before going we'd want to be knowing
whether in-flight-movies would be showing!

Comic-book fare of danger and dare
and a superhero beyond compare,
Heralded a birth and a rich worth
of movies about a powerful surf,
Obediently blind he served mankind
with superpowers that did spellbind,
No joins were seen on the big widescreen
which for *Superman* was a perfect means,
The tagline cry was truly no lie,
we really believed that a man can fly,
And no mistaking the world was handshaking
Christopher Reeve – a star in the making.

Without furore but worthy of glory
where do I begin to tell the *Love Story*
of Ali McGraw who closed fame's door
to nurse Steve McQueen her dying amour,
A very short fad was daughter and dad
Ryan and Tatum who weren't so bad,
One's cup of tea but not for me
was Glenda Jackson who became an MP!
Light and frothy and tasty as toffee
Farrah Fawcett was my cuppa coffee.

There's nothing that Barbra Streisand has lacked
she can dance, sing, act, and is nicely stacked,
Her records shifted because she's gifted
and her music fans were always uplifted,
Subtle and deep suited Meryl Streep
who proved it true some could act in their sleep,
But this acting ace and woman of grace
caused Barbra Striesand to 'watch this space',
For Meryl's career broke a frontier
when she later appeared in *Mamma Mia.*

A script all shot, cast and crew on pot
and Francis Ford Coppola losing the plot,
but yet somehow *Apocalypse Now*
became a revered cult film – and how!
Mohican haircuts caused blood and guts
in *Taxi Driver* which was the mutt's nuts,
But the bees-knees about Mob trustees
was of course *The Godfather,* if you please,
this film for sure pioneered a couture
for stylish violence with polished allure,
its rave reviews and golden statues
made us an offer we couldn't refuse.

Dirty Harry didn't need to marry
'cos on his forefinger he did carry
the metallic ring of firearm bling,
a .45 magnum made his day zing.

Goodbye fig leaves, cue *Deep Throat* sleaze,
the best money-maker since Adam and Eve,
it raised applause from sweaty paws
by dirty old men in raincoats indoors,
The 70's best for artistic quest
concerned the habits of a seagoing pest,
Jaws has become, especially for some,
the reason why films can be one's best chum,
Add to this adage the *Star Wars* package;
a moviedom must and rite of passage.
(Though please let me stress with a quick P.S.
that's the first three films not the later mess.)

This decade heard the Blockbuster word
and also the names: Scorsese and Spielberg,
The saviour had landed, a name was branded,
Hollywood's reins to the Auteur were handed,
Would this affect us? Just to correct us
that movies were now owned by directors!
This brilliant perk let directors work
without the bother of a studio jerk,
Whatever their mission Auteurs had vision,
then Michael Cimino caused bad frisson,
Cimino lost trust through his power lust;
his *Heaven's Gate* saw a studio go bust,
Taking back power to their ivory tower
something else made the studios cower,
The decade's conclusion had more confusion
as Video jockeyed for its inclusion.

THE EIGHTIES

"I'm an actor. An actress is someone who wears boa feathers."
Sigourney Weaver.

This decade saw, hitting the hard floor,
the slackening of many a gobsmacked jaw,
We had to console the hard earned goal
of B-movie talent in an all time role,
Some said "okay," others "no way,"
for President Reagan of the USA,
Deplored or adored what can't be ignored,
the wall came down and the cold war thawed,
It's maybe a factor his charm helped capture
this order along with another actor,
It earned not a scoff nor shouts of "get off"
when Looking For Freedom was sung by the Hoff.

Forget banality; onto reality
of those who aid film's popularity,
We gave good thanks to good guy pranks
from wholesome, humorous, humble Tom Hanks,
Michael J. Fox showed how he rocks
without being one of life's rippling jocks,
The son of Kirk had a *Wall Street* smirk
when Michael Douglas proclaimed greed worked,
Mel Gibson showed to heed the code
that a *Lethal Weapon* can often explode,
Showing great soul, Jeff Bridges' main goal
was shunning star turns for a meaty role,
For smooth as silk with his fast talking bilk
very few ever matched James Woods' ilk,
Except comic Aesop and over the top
fab Eddie Murphy the *Beverley Hills Cop*.

Great craftsmanship helped to equip
a hero who cracked a mean bull-whip,
To face uncertainties on dark journeys
that aped serial films of the 1930's,
In a leather trilby and nicknamed Indy
Indiana Jones showed what and will be,
With relative modesty and laconically
as professor of history and archaeology,
He caused real sparks seeking lost arks
but the one time he truly earned top-marks,
Was lifting the gloom in temples of doom
by denying the Nazis any elbowroom,
The last crusade was his last parade
when plans for retiring were justly made,
With foes defeated and scripts depleted
to slippers and armchair he retreated.

Kev Costner's break was cowboy Jake
and what an impression he did make,
from *Silverado* to his own argot
of *Dancing With Wolves* which earned a BRAVO!
With teen-idol zeal, Tom Cruise's appeal
was that he was born to perform on reel,
Stallone the croak, Arnold the oak
and muscle-man Van Damme were action bespoke,
But beating them all, Bruce Willis stood tall
in a sweaty T-shirt and *Die Hard* brawl,
An equal achiever, Sigourney Weaver
had an admirer who wouldn't leave her,
a name amassed for this statuesque lass
through kicking a pissed-off *Alien*'s ass,
Ditto *Rambo* who made a BANG go
but in the end he turned into panto.

Treading the boards and winning awards
she rose to become one of film's great broads,
a debut at two, through custard pies true,
then hooking at fourteen brought a breakthrough,
now Jodie Foster dines on lobster
and talent is all that it has cost her,
Hot Kathleen Turner became a big earner
through *Body Heat* and her female purdah,
Whilst Goldie Hawn was mainly drawn
to humorous heroines much less torn,
Breaking a leg an actress called Meg
reached a climax and earned a nest egg.

Built like a haystack, in sunglasses-black,
he made the prediction "I'll be back!"
forget Darth Vader, nothing was greater
than the one known as *The Terminator*,
Though coming close but more verbose
Manhunter gave us someone as gross,
A Doctor was he but the world could see
Hannibal Lector failed humanity,
On the good side how much we cried,
for *The Elephant Man* who tried to hide,
Another one too whose looks on us grew;
ET was the one who made us boo hoo!

Codpieces galore struck a rapport
in *Amadeus* which was top drawer,
Without a codpiece the 80's *Grease*
was *Dirty Dancing* and Swayze's showpiece,
Much less aloof with maladroit truth
This is Spinal Tap was the ultimate spoof,
Fantasy was never ever more clever
than *The Princess Bride*, a favourite forever,

But beating its chest and the 80's rest
is *Raging Bull*, a celluloid best.

When thinking of cult we best consult
Blade runner as the one we all exult,
A welcome flux for movie schmucks
saw other cult classics take our bucks,
Scots accent aside (which caused a divide)
The Highlander was a thrilling ride,
The manic pace and hilarious chase
of *Raising Arizona* was just as ace,
Never to be scoffed, hats are doffed
to *Airplane* and *Ferris Buellers Day Off*,
Whilst many confess that they feel blessed
for *Back To The Future*, a trilogy best.

When friends are pally should they dally?
enquired the movie *When Harry Met Sally*,
More open and frank and drama top-rank
the low-budget hit and carnal think-tank,
Sex Lies And Videotape helped create
'Indie' productions which opened the gate,
For there now to be most welcomingly
a bullish new Indiewood industry,
And one to trust as a festival must
for those with a burning creative lust,
Was sunny Utah where progress saw
the Sundance film fest become a big draw,
Where finding a share for low budget fare
has a real chance of getting an air,
Artistic candour is its mantra,
to showcase talent – not extravaganza,
And lending his ear whom we hold dear
is Robert Redford, film festival seer.

THE NINETIES

"I wouldn't do nudity in films. For me, personally... to act with my clothes on is a performance; to act with my clothes off is a documentary."
Julia Roberts

The 90's start produced great art
with the weepie *Ghost*, a film with a heart,
The decade's end then had the godsend
of *The Sixth Sense* – a ghostly bookend!
Beauty And The Beast was such a feast
The Lion King too, to say the least,
Then evolution saw revolution
through CGI and its FX solution,
It made its mark with *Jurassic Park*
but the best of all for adventurous lark?
Cowboy Woody and Buzz his buddy
were lightyears ahead of the usual goodie,
the screen was lit with urbane wit
as *Toy Story* proved a blockbuster hit,
we struck a bond of characters fond
of box-office infinity and beyond.

Did *Pretty Woman* try to help rid
a hooker's stigma from being sordid?
Never uncouth but sweet as vermouth,
how prettied-up lies hide the ugly truth,
But Hollywood's thing is let's put a spin
on what can make the tills go kerching!
Cue *Forrest Gump* which brought a lump
to the throat of many a cynical chump,
Yet for all its faults deep within its vault
cinema has moments that scar and jolt.

The work of directors can connect us
with well-told stories that so affect us,
Pick your own from Oliver Stone;
cue his Vietnam trilogy warzone,
And Spielberg's gravitas is of such class
his *Schindler's List* earned him a pass
to Oscar acclaim for the Holocaust shame
which showed man as loving and inhumane,
Like the compelling perhaps excelling
Saving Private Ryan which had eyes welling.

Often an attraction to a large faction
is mindless violence coupled with action,
And what often hogs film internet blogs
are cult *Pulp Fiction* and *Reservoir Dogs,*
Hail Tarantino and the film beano
of *Goodfellas, Heat* and *Casino,*
And *Fargo* too, they all really knew
how to offer what folks would want to view,
For trendy violence coupled with science
The Matrix delivered for its clients,
So could we say of the bullet buffet
in *Terminator 2: Judgement Day,*
The violent craft at which we laughed
was *Mars Attack* which was loveably daft,
But for scaring mams and babies in prams
nothing beats *Silence Of The Lambs.*

How less incensed we all felt against
women who violence on men dispensed!
Scriptwriter pens had focused the lens
on a film that saw cocks lose to hens,
As the T-bird flies, "No" were the cries
when *Thelma And Louise* said their goodbyes.

Hail John Travolta who did not falter
on his last chance at the comeback altar,
Pulp Fiction ensured his career was cured
and Samuel L. Jackson's fame was inured,
Though Billy Crystal carried no pistol
he fired puns quickest and by the fistful,
But the main man with fists that can
move quicker than lightning is Jackie Chan,
Cameron Diaz has the pizzazz
to make men make fists, oh yes she has!
and sales of hair-gel improved like hell
when applied to the hair of this gorgeous belle.

The transoceanic ill-fated *Titanic*
needed a maverick and someone dynamic,
to some it sucks but they're just schmucks
'cos like it or not, it made megabucks,
and raising the bar was film-making star
Jim Cameron who earned his kingly HOORAH!

The Shawshank Redemption without exemption
is a film that fans all fondly mention,
its intelligence plain and treat for the brain
makes it worth seeing again and again,
But was there ever a film more clever
than *Groundhog Day*? No, I think never!
But was there ever a film more clever
than *Groundhog Day*? No, I think never!
But was there ever a film more...

Film's unsung pal who forever shall
be an acting best is Robert Duvall,
The two who emit ultra-cool and wit
are Johnny Depp and, of course, Brad Pitt,

Of the same class but with added panache
is gorgeous George and his debonair dash,
Without compare for looks and flair
Denzel Washington is right up there,
As is Will Smith who did forthwith
mature as a 'leading man' monolith.

Whether bent cops or renaissance fops
give actors a chance and their acting chops,
Will without shame profit their gain
by chewing the scenery, frame by frame,
Cue the gung-ho, butch Russell Crowe
and Daniel Day Lewis who's just as macho,
Uphill, downhill, bitter pill, through the mill,
Robert Downey Junior fits the bill,
In a lighter role each scene she stole,
that's Whoopie Goldberg whom we extol,
Ditto old hand from cloud cuckoo land
Robin Williams who's a matchless brand.

From comedy learner to multi faced gurner
Jim Carrey became a big money earner,
Another way known is to have flesh shown
cue admiration for brave Sharon Stone,
Without doing nude, Julia Roberts wooed
'till a 'highest-paid' title had accrued,
Men have oft snuck much more than a look
at Michelle Pfeiffer and Sandra Bullock,
Beyond the bleachers Kate Winslet's features
marked her as one of film's *Heavenly Creatures*,
And Angelina Jolie is someone surely
who with her charms can heal the poorly,
she played a toft called Lara Croft
and then her career took off aloft.

To define a Star one needn't look far
to one who deserved to get the cigar,
Both a Don Juan and a Peter Pan,
Warren Beatty had all one ever can,
This man about town surrendered his crown
when at last he finally settled down,
There's no disputing that his seducing
is something that men don't mind saluting,
A truer ambition brought no fruition
for he didn't become a politician,
Though ask any dame and they will claim
his conquests shame Bill Clinton's fame!

From the clapperboard's clap and run of a lap
to the finishing line of "it's a wrap,"
From slapstick humour to fighting a tumour,
whether based on truth, lies or a rumour,
From no fanfare to an epic premiere,
whether humble indie or franchised affair,
From film maniacs to cynical hacks,
whether in an art house or a grand IMAX,
Whilst eating nibbles the screenwriter's scribbles
helps us forget life's annoying quibbles,
And forever we'll craze idling our days
berating turkeys or lavishing praise,
'Cos whatever their grade films will be made
and money for tickets will always be paid,
But then causing doubt was HBO's clout
which saw staying-in as the new going-out,
And another threat making studios sweat
was the one coming from the Internet,
Initially crude it led to YouTube
and big Porno sales along with lube,
But don't condemn just carpe diem
because if you can't beat them join 'em!

ABOVE LEFT: An early day travelling lantern showman (lanternist) carrying his equipment, as well as a drum for sound effects. **ABOVE RIGHT:** It wasn't Marlon Brando but Eadweard Muybridge who was the true Godfather of motion pictures.

BELOW LEFT: Edison's Kinetoscope. **BELOW RIGHT:** Mark Buck in the control room at VUE, Hull, where information is keyed into a 10-Terabyte server computer, allowing over 100 movies to be stored at any one time with transfer between 10 projectors programmable remotely from a laptop.

TOM MIX

(WHO IS APPEARING AT THE PALACE THEATRE ALL THIS WEEK).
BEING WELCOMED ON HIS ARRIVAL IN HULL BY
"BUDDY McSHERRY" and "PALEFACE LA PRAIRIE"
in their COWBOY and INDIAN SUITS

FROM

WILLIS'S

TOY FAIR

Willis's have a full range of COWBOY and INDIAN SUITS and accessories,
at prices to suit all.

One of these Suits will make an IDEAL XMAS GIFT for any child —
and of course they are equally suitable for Children's Fancy Dress Parties.

COWBOY SUITS	INDIAN SUITS	TOMAHAWKS 1/- each
All complete from	Complete from	TOM-TOMS 3/11 each
5/11 to 29/6	5/11 to 16/11	TENTS 12/11 and 18/11
		CAMP FIRES 5/11

CARR LANE **WILLIS'S** CITY SQUARE

LEFT: Tom mix arrives in Hull in 1938, to be met by two young fans in their 'Cowboy and Indian suits' purchased from Willis's department store, which is now a Primark outlet.

BELOW: In 2010 Captain Jack Sparrow (Johnny Depp) arrives with two of his shipmates holding a letter written by 9-year-old pirate fan Beatrice Delap, who asked for tips on how to mutiny at school.

ABOVE: 70 years after it was bombed in the Hull blitz of March 1941, the National Picture Theatre is proving to be the cinema that just won't die.

BELOW: A cinema institution that never bombed and whose memory will never die... Laurel and Hardy are dined out by Hull Cinema Managers Society in 1947, chaired by Everard Jordan, front row far right. Ida Laurel is front row left, Lucille Hardy is front row right. The last piece of British soil that Stan and Ollie ever stood on was in Hull, before returning by ship to the USA in 1954.

ABOVE: The Tower Picture Palace, Hull, Yorkshire.
BELOW: Crowds at Grauman's Chinese Theatre, Hollywood Boulevard.

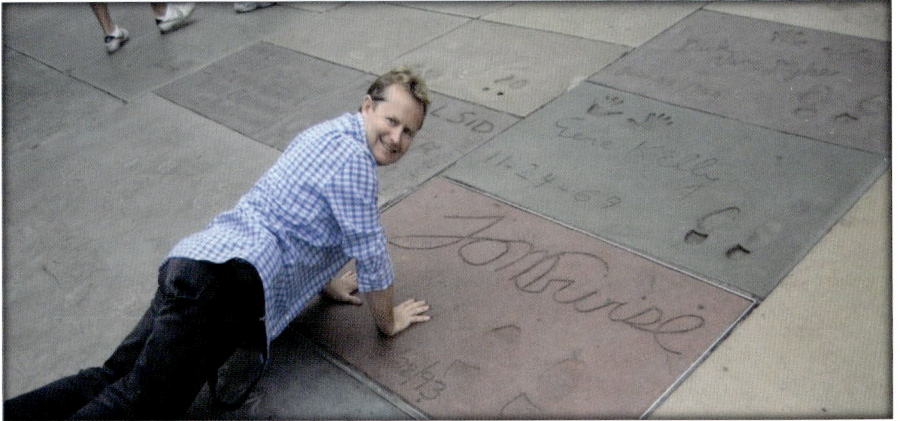

ABOVE: The Forecourt of Imortality at Grauman's Chinese Theatre and a fan looking to follow in the footsteps of Tom Cruise!

BELOW LEFT: A brilliant wax likeness of Marilyn Monroe at Madame Tussuads on Hollywood Boulevard, which portrays her signing her name in wet cement.

BELOW: Marilyn Monroe's actual hand and footprints made in 1953. To the left of Marilyn at the same ceremony was brunette Jane Russell. The words written across both of their squares read: ***Gentlemen Prefer Blondes***

ABOVE: Whilst Gene Autry is the only artist honoured with a star in all five categories on the Walk Of Fame (Television, Radio, Music, Theatre and Film), Mickey Mouse's star sums up for many what Hollywood is all about!

BELOW: Is heaven waking up to the Pearly Gates, working for Bill Gates, or walking through the Paramount Gates? Founded in 1912, Paramount is America's oldest running movie studio and the only remaining major studio actually in Hollywood. As such it is also the only major studio that can truthfully state in the credits of any movie it produces: 'Made In Hollywood'.

ABOVE LEFT: A bronze statue on Hollywood Boulevard of legendary Charlie Chaplin.

ABOVE RIGHT: A bronze statue of the equally legendary Buster Keaton, also located on Hollywood Boulevard.

LEFT: When your face appears in Hollywood on a billboard, you know you have made it. But when your face appears on a billboard on the side of a skyscraper in Hollywood, you *really* know you have made it!

TOP: Sir Tom Courtenay and me in our younger days.

MIDDLE: Omar Sharif and me in our older days.

RIGHT: Julie Christie (but without me) in her youth, who was and still is the embodiment of a screen goddess on any given day.

CELEBRITY

"Being famous has its benefits but fame isn't one of them."
Larry Wall

"I'm no paragon," said Susan Sarandon
but she is a valued liberal banner man,
an Eastwick witch though never a bitch,
she believed in more than just being rich,
forgetting career she fought without fear
for all the just causes that she held dear,
Also imbued, Tim Robbins pursued
along with Sean Penn the same attitude,
Above parapets some at least put necks
without much care for big pay day cheques.

By whatever means some must have their dreams
in Hollywood where all isn't what it seems,
The 'Me Me Me' star celebrity
demanding a million-dollar fee,
Not all, but some, they soon become
enslaved to the showbiz rule-of-thumb,
A fancy zipcode for one's abode,
with access gained by a private road,
Career arrangers, personal trainers,
an entourage of 'yes' men on retainers,
Chauffeurs, fans, name in Grauman's,
house-maids to clean one's pots and pans,
Talk shows, premieres, Oscar tears,
praises being sung by fawning peers,
A nip and tuck, hair that stays stuck,
finding an agent who isn't a crook,
Demanding the script that's hotly tipped
as a sure-fire-winning box-office hit.

"Can you not spot that I'm so hot,
I'm a big superstar and you are not!"
Often you'll find such thoughts in the mind
of those who think they're a special kind,
The kind who conceive and truly believe
it's rarefied air that they now breathe,
Yet what they've gotten can be so rotten
'cos their scandals ain't easily forgotten,
Their so-called fame is public domain
which often serves to entertain,
A messy divorce can follow a course
more gripping than any film tour-de-force,
A sly sex session indiscretion,
drink or drugs or involved in aggression,
Without sympathy the press with glee
exists to expose the celeb dynasty,
That risk celebs take when seeking a break
for work in a business they know is fake,
Their belief you see is: "That just won't be,
I'm never gonna let that happen to me."

He walked the walk and talked the talk
he had it all did Mickey Rourke,
In his wisdom he bucked the system
which lost him his way, his pull and income,
His demons within put him in a spin
the old King was dead, long live the King,
His way of detoxing was taking-up boxing
which somehow became his way of outfoxing,
The Hollywood game and pressure of fame
to which he confessed was all his own blame,
He shed no tears, then in later years
he made a comeback with cauliflower ears.

21ST CENTURY CINEMA AND BEYOND

"In America it's considered a lot more important to be a great Batman than a great Hamlet."
Kevin Kline

The Noughties began with a big loud bang
but this was the noise of the unified pan,
for the awful dearth of *Battlefield Earth*
but at least it had some comedic worth,
Restoring faith, one can vouchsafe
Gladiator's lustre which caused a strafe,
Of big storyboards of sandals and swords
like *Troy* and *Alexander* – epic war lords,
Biopics pay and holding sway
were *Capote, Ali, Milk,* and *Ray,*
Also admired was the much desired
Erin Brockovich who truly inspired,
And folks patronised a President's rise
in *W.* which turned out a hit surprise.

In 2003 the world did see
a subdued 75th anniversary,
Of Oscar awards promo billboards
when US and UK marauding hordes,
Went on to attack the land of Iraq,
an action thought an illegal Bush-whack,
Politics aside we mustn't deride
film's big annual sycophantic ride,
How it feels good to have once stood
on the world's biggest stage called Hollywood,
Where egos are fed not with water or bread
but with worship and awe – alive or dead,
For an Oscar's meant to represent
the ultimate honour in big screen ascent,

Thus players crave on their way to the grave
the glory it gives for all that they gave.

Lord Of The Rings gave cinema things
and earned itself eleven Oscar wins,
The magic swotter called Harry Potter
went from hot to being hotter,
Star War plans saw Sith hit the fans
with a prequel trilogy of warring gangs,
The Pirates Of The Caribbean
is a series demanding we all see' em,
they can't run fallow with Cap'n Jack Sparrow
a cinematic wonder whom we should hallow.

A revelation was *Lost in Translation*
and *The Wrestler* also found elation,
Borat the prat was no diplomat,
Disney's *Enchanted* was thankfully that,
Somewhat forlorn a genre was born
when *Hostel* and *Saw* brought torture porn,
Genres mattered and profits were shattered
when zany zombies' guts were splattered,
Vampires as well had a healthy spell
of heroes trying to send them to hell,
For perfect skin and the 'fashion thing'
along came the genre of movie bling,
New York vistas and Jimmy Choo blisters
pleased *Sex And The City* fashionistas,
Any promenader with couture ardour
also lapped up *The Devil Wears Prada,*
Earning the dough and surprisingly so
documentaries often stole the show,
and one to cite that's a sheer delight,
is *March Of The Penguins* and their life plight.

DVD's rise saw VHS die
whilst hand-drawn was losing to CGI,
And animation touched the nation
with *The Incredibles* who were a sensation,
A fairytale treat that's truly complete
is *Shrek* with its send-up that's hard to beat,
But fond affection without exemption
for a family film that's near perfection,
is the no-way trash, shy and the flash,
WALL: E and Eve who cleaned up the cash,
And standing apart with its teary start
was *Up* that hands-down won everyone's heart.

Coming to blows against fiends and foes
we can always rely on comic-book heroes,
The man of steel still proved a big deal,
Superman Returns confirmed his appeal,
No foe or rampart could ever outsmart
New York's wall-crawler with the big heart,
just who's not a fan of *Spiderman*
and wished they could webhop like he can?
No rubber-suit but a hell of a hoot
saw *Iron Man* scoop-up box-office loot,
How *The Dark Knight* to the Joker's delight
gave countless children a hell of a fright,
Though more of a shock was when the tick-tock
tragically stopped on Heath Ledger's clock!

With jokes to crack, cue the Frat Pack
with Wilson, Ferrell, Carell and Black,
And no pan-handler or comic Cassandra
is the contradiction Adam Sandler,
Since being *The Jerk* we laughed and smirked
(Pink Panther aside) at Steve Martin's work,

The comic pillar now handling the tiller
is a day in the laugh of fun Ben Stiller.

Fans became fond of a darker James Bond
with Daniel Craig the fair haired blonde,
In his old age and for less of a wage
Kevin Spacey hit the London stage,
Sean Penn attested he couldn't be bested
at least when he wasn't being arrested,
For Zac Efron the spotlight shone
and Dicaprio lost the teen baton,
Torn *Jason Bourne* had Matt Damon's brawn,
J Lo and Ben just made us all yawn,
For stealing the stage with demonic rage
cue Gary Oldman and Nicolas Cage,
For manic craze the bar was raised
by Christian Bale's profane strangeways,
But nought could outsell the rants of Mel
in a kiss and tell from the depths of hell.

A Bond girl cutie and ultra beauty
gained Halle Berry Hollywood's booty,
Charlize Theron was right on song,
as an ugly *Monster* a gong came along,
Lit-up in neon is empyrean
Nicole Kidman the Antipodean,
Cate Blanchett too is an Aussie who
is worth a blow on the didgeridoo,
As is the glitz, the youth looks and wits
of Cruz, Fox and Alba who have nice bits,
Of the old broads still treading the boards
Keaton and Bening can still win awards,
But it must be said for acting street-cred
Meryl Streep leaves all the rest for dead.

Other famous gemstones dragging old bones
are Nicholson, Ford and Tommy Lee Jones,
Never a demon or ever a he-man
but ever distinguished is Morgan Freeman,
A white shark's fins to an angel's wings
goes the range of Sir Anthony Hopkins,
But the rugged feller standing stellar
both as an actor and storyteller
is last name Eastwood, first name Clint,
a legend who's left his iconic imprint.

What a feeling to break the glass ceiling,
Kathryn Bigelow was joyfully reeling,
History was made and a debt was paid
for as Best Director she'd made the grade,
The Hurt Locker showed and it bestowed
that women in movies aren't overshadowed.

The decade ended, rules were upended
and James Cameron we all befriended,
Like General Custer he had to muster
troops to defend his maverick blockbuster,
But what you'll swear is "yes, I was there,"
for *Avatar* and its grand premiere,
Call it poetry in motion capture,
the height of how movies can enrapture,
And this technology discovery
meant the rest, as they say, was history.

History has clout and *The King's Speech* shout
was that simple drama can still win out,
No special effects, loud bangs or sex,
yet this low-cost indie earned world respect,
For truth was the trick to this biopic
which proved we still love an old-fashioned flick.

A MOVIE'S COMMON DENOMINATOR

"Love affairs have always greatly interested me but I do not greatly care for them in books or moving pictures. In a love affair I wish to be the hero, with no audience present."
E W Howe

For better or worse, money in a purse
will always win between art v commerce,
But not to be slated, cinema created
a medium that has constantly sated,
Upon much queuing followed by viewing,
for a century movies have been wooing,
For folks to pay and find their way
to a flip-up seat where one daresay,
They might connect with a film's subject
that'll hopefully have a profound effect,
Take for example the many ample
'rags to riches' stories to sample,
There Will Be Blood both drilled and dug
to make The American Dream come good,
Revolutionary Road bluntly showed
how such a dream can also corrode,
For every filmgoer a true hornblower
of America's Dream is *Rocky Balboa!*

Yet the best seen American Dream
was surely the one played off the screen,
The true life drama of Barack Obama
who helped the States re-find its nirvana,
But it's not about America's clout
the lives of others are worth a shout,
And *Slumdog Millionaire* showed we care
for other folks dreams, however threadbare.

Though some complained a genre was stained
when a western norm was re-arranged,
Westerns hold sway with something to say
'bout men being men and not being gay,
But turning a cheek, so to speak,
Brokeback Mountain confirmed a mystique,
Up on the screen runs an endless seam
regardless whatever is a film's theme,
It's that we depend on love to help mend
and what are all films about in the end?
Fresh or hoary, failure or glory,
films are all really just a love story.

THE END

THAT'S ALL FOLKS

FIN

Well, not quite...

AND THE WINNER IS...

*"People say I pay too much attention to the look of a movie.
But for God's sake, I'm not producing a Radio 4 Play for
Today, I'm making a movie that people are going to look at."*
Ridley Scott

Films now and then with zeitgeist and Zen
can earn a just score of ten out of ten,
And raising the bar easily by far
was *The Social Network*, my last HURRAH!
But the Facebook page for a bygone age
has been the flicks not an internet rage,
So note before ending, I'll be spending
my time and money whilst I'm attending,
Films at the flicks where nothing else licks
getting my quota of celluloid kicks.

What other medium breaks the tedium
and helps us escape like balloons of helium,
On a long flight to face a great fight
where guys get the girl and wrongs are put right?
Or as can unfurl in this changing world
the guy gets the guy and girl gets the girl!
Then journey complete and foe well beat
before we finally vacate our seat,
Acknowledging laughter or maybe tears,
up there on the screen allaying life's fears,
Is the great cliché reaching up to the rafter:
"And they all lived happily ever after."

...especially if the movie wins an Oscar or a Bafta!

PART TWO

GOING TO THE CINEMA – A PERSONAL REFLECTION

A popcorn treat in a cinema seat
and a blockbuster film makes life complete.

PICTURE PALACES, PICTURE PEOPLE
AND PICTURE PARAPHERNALIA.

Quentin Tarantino said at the 2005 Empire awards show in London: "My plan is to have a movie theatre in some small town. I'll be the manager, this crazy old movie guy. I've made enough money that nobody even needs to show up... it's just having something to do. I will make little speeches before each movie. That sounds like a pretty cool life."

Tarantino's retirement plan is also a life that I would like, only not in some small town. Instead, I'd choose Grauman's Chinese Theatre on Hollywood Boulevard, where I performed in what I coined its Forecourt of Immortality.

Of all the movie venues ever built, the Chinese Theatre is the most well known and for me it is the holy grail of picture palaces. This fabulously opulent picture palace, with its original seating capacity of 2,258, was based on Chinese art, architecture and culture. On 18 May 1927, Sid Grauman, the main shareholder in the Chinese Theatre, hosted its grand opening. The premiere that night was Cecil B. DeMille's *King Of Kings* and the billing read: Sid Grauman   Cecil B. DeMille   Jesus Christ – in that order!

It has since held the record for hosting more premieres than any other movie theatre in the world. Yet it's not the theatre's stunning architecture or the movies shown that has the crowds visiting in their thousands! The major draw is to check out the imprints of the hands and feet left by movie stars in wet cement in the theatre's public forecourt. (The first movie premiere I saw there in 2001 was *Captain Corelli's Mandolin*. It was preceded by the star of the film, Nicholas Cage, receiving the honour of leaving his hands and feet imprints. Though I would like to think he felt just as honoured from any impression I may have made when giving him a firm Yorkshire handshake as the Hollywood Town Crier, especially as I didn't criticise the accent he used in the film!)

One legend how this tradition originated is that in 1927 when the chief foreman, Jean Klossner, finished the construction of the forecourt he knelt down by a poster frame and placed his right-hand print in wet cement along with his initials, J.W.K., which remain today. Another legend is that during a construction visit, actress Norma Talmadge accidentally stepped into a sidewalk of wet cement. This was witnessed by the theatre's owner Sid Grauman and the rest, as they say, is history.

The inaugural hand and footprint ceremony on the 30 April 1927 featured the silent era's golden couple, Douglas Fairbanks and Mary Pickford. Norma Talmadge followed later. As well as leaving imprints of hands and feet, along with signing their names some added a short message. Sylvester Stallone wrote "Keep punching America," Arnold Schwarzenegger warned "I'll be back" and Clint Eastwood declared "You made my day!"

Some inductees expressed themselves in other ways and visitors can see the imprints of: Al Jolson's knees, Harold Lloyd's spectacles, the cigars of Groucho Marks and George Burns, Betty Grable's legs, the noses of Jimmy Durante and Bob Hope, the tread marks of R2D2, the dreadlocks of Whoopi Goldberg, the guns of William S. Hart and Roy Rogers, and John Wayne's fist.

A question that I heard visitors ask was: "How on earth can someone like Adam Sandler appear but Charlie Chaplin doesn't?" This is because the concrete block with Chaplin's imprints was removed in the 1950's due to his left-wing political views. This fact and hundreds of others are given greater mention in several comprehensive books. My own contribution to the Chinese Theatre's standing comes in the form of a poem, which I wrote and orated to tourists.

THE FORECOURT OF IMMORTALITY

Aristocratic Hollywood sign –

A loved and revered grand old dame,

Oscar nights and movie premieres,

Or a shiny star on the Walk of Fame,

These eminent icons and institutions,

Showcase Hollywood's history book,

But it's to Grauman's Chinese Theatre,

Where millions come to stand and look,

At a tradition which proves the movies,

Can empower through the silver screen,

Celebrity status, more grand and royal,

Than that of a Prince, a King or a Queen,

Greater than that of a President,

A luminary's legend can live on,

More than in painting, poetry and prose,

More than in sculpture, stories or song,

And undoubtedly the best testament,

To those remembered with admiring stares,

Are the hand and footprints of film's elite,

In blocks of silent, cold concrete squares.

Also appearing beside several cowboy stars are the hoof prints of Gene Autry's horse, Champion, Roy Rogers' horse, Trigger, and Tom Mix's horse, Tony. In memory of my dad, it was the latter of these three cowboys that I sought out before any other name on my first visit to the Chinese Theatre in 1999.

"Tom Mix would never have stood for it!" That's what my dad used to say when he was exasperated, bemused, or mad as hell. Tom Mix may sound familiar to some of you and others won't have a clue who he is. Yet anyone interested in popular culture might not realise that they have seen his picture many times. Along with Marlon Brando, Laurel and Hardy and Marilyn Monroe, his Stetson adorned face gazes out from the cover of the Beatles album Sgt Pepper's Lonely Hearts Club Band. Mix was a silent movie and early talkies cowboy actor and a true megastar. It was almost a generation since he had passed away when he was chosen by the 'Fab Four' to appear on the world's greatest album cover.

Mix made over 300 films between 1910 and 1935, and all but nine were silent features. In real life he was a champion rodeo rider and carried out his own daring stunts. These skills helped him become the top cowboy star of his day earning a staggering $10,000 a week. Wearing fancy western outfits and employing an upright code of ethics, Mix's squeaky-clean image was often spoofed in later years. (An affectionate portrayal of Tom Mix by Bruce Willis can be seen in the 1988 film Sunset.) Back in the silent era and then later with his equally famous horse in the early talkies, Mix was the original movie hero for millions of cinema going children – one of whom was my dad.

My dad's schooling in the twenties and thirties was something he didn't take kindly to. In 1933 at the age of 10, together with a couple of pals, he raided penny coins from the school gas-meter. With their new found wealth they paid for the best seats and refreshments at the Star cinema. This was a much loved venue in the small town of Hessle just outside the city of Hull, where the authorities quickly cottoned-on that kids dressed in rags, sitting in the best balcony seats and gleefully licking on an ice-cream in each hand had been funded by something more than rarely given pocket money.

My grandmother assured the police it wouldn't happen again and "anyway it was the movies that were corrupting the children" she proclaimed in my dad's defence. Though dad was now banned from the Star cinema in Hessle, there was another cinema called the Eureka several miles away on the long road to Hull. In the twenties and thirties kids would walk shoeless to the end of the world to find what limited entertainment there was. Dad was no different and the Eureka became the spot for his childhood escapism. (The Star mysteriously burned to the ground a year or so later!)

When silents changed to talkies, the popularity of westerns slumped for a while and parts began drying up for Mix. But ever the showman, he took his screen antics on the road and toured in a Wild West themed show – The Tom Mix Circus. This included a visit to Britain and, more importantly, a visit to Hull.

In September 1938, he had top billing at Hull's Palace Theatre and his entourage was stabled in an area which now boasts a brand-spanking-new bus station. During his stay he decided to go for a ride and he galloped his horse, Tony, through the city and on to the road leading to Hessle. His first stop was the Wassand Arms pub where he rode through its big double doors to have a pint with astonished locals. Blazing a trail further along Hessle Road and cheered on by excited crowds, he reached the Eureka cinema. He steered Tony up the steps into the auditorium. The gasps and cheers of the Saturday matinee kids all crammed inside nearly took the roof off. To see 'Marshal Mix' astride his mount blasting away on his six guns right there in the flesh was beyond any young kid's

71

imagination. And, of course, who was there to witness this unbelievable spectacle, everyone but my dad!

Dad had joined up in 1938 and a year later, on declaration of war he was trained for active service. In 1940 he was shipped out to India. From there as part of the elite Chindits fighting force, he went on to fight the Japanese in Burma. In that same year a sprightly sixty-year-old Tom Mix was killed in a freak one-car auto accident in the US. Mix's head almost came off when a suitcase flew off the rear shelf of his single-seated roadster as it plunged into a gulley on an Arizona highway.

Dad survived the war with his head intact, unlike some of his pals who fell afoul of Japanese war atrocities. For the remainder of his days dad spoke great ill of the Japanese but glowingly of Tom Mix.

I have always thought that a television breaks up the monotony of looking at a home's drab painted walls and a cinema breaks up the monotony of looking at every town's drab high streets. In 1990, the Eureka in Hull changed business to become a bingo hall. Falling bingo audiences then saw it close for good in 1996. In 2005, having fallen into total disrepair, it was demolished and is now a car park for a LIDL supermarket. "Tom Mix would never have stood for it," as dad would say.

The equivalent of the old double feature at the cinema was like going into a pub and being restricted to having only two pints, usually a quality pint accompanied by a lesser one. The modern day equivalent of visiting a multiplex cinema is like going into a pub and having as many quality pints as you want, although there is still a chance of a lesser one. Many modern day cinemas now have more screens in one multiplex than the total number of cinemas in some British towns or cities prior to World War Two (WW2). However, it would take a large multiplex to beat the amount of cinemas in Hull, which was often described as Cinema City.

The port city of Hull in the county of Yorkshire is not noted for its climes of warm days and balmy nights. Chilly eastern winds blow in off the North Sea, whilst the tail-end of Atlantic rain clouds float in from over the Pennines in the west. However, this did not deter Hull town-planners building the first open air cinema in Britain. Named the Garden Cinema, it opened for business in the July of 1912 and closed ready for the onset of winter – to never open again. During 1912-1935 nine other picture houses had opened and closed still leaving an astonishing 35 cinemas for its 200,000 filmgoers by the outbreak of WW2 in 1939.

A not so well known fact outside of Hull is that the city endured the first daylight raid of the war and the last piloted air raid. Between 1939 and 1945 Hull was bombed 82 times resulting in 1,200 killed and thousands injured. It is said of the 191,660 homes in the city, fewer than 6,000 survived undamaged with some 152,000 people rendered homeless at one time or another! Hull was second only to London for war damage but, due to strict reporting by the Government, when reports of bombing raids were mentioned the city was often referred to only as "a north-east coast town."

An even lesser known fact outside of Hull is that relentless bombing in the blitz of 1941 caused the destruction of six cinemas across the city. One of the popular cinemas destroyed was the National Picture Theatre, which opened in December 1914 on Beverley Road. It closed after a bombing raid in March 1941, when ironically the film showing was Charlie Chaplin's satire on Hitler: *The Great Dictator*. On hearing the air raid sirens an audience of 150 couldn't escape outside due to falling bombs and were all saved by taking shelter in the cinema foyer. The falling bombs completely gutted the interior, although the foyer and building façade remarkably survived. In February 2007 the cinema was recognised for its historic importance by the Department of Culture, Media and Sport, and awarded Grade II listing. Apart from a few churches it is allegedly the only civilian building in Europe to be blitzed during the war which remains in exactly the same condition today.

At the time of writing, The National Civilian WW2 Memorial Trust is hoping to raise £750,000 to preserve the site in memory of victims of the blitz and the people who served on the Home Front. Plans have been drawn up to turn the site into an educational and tourism facility, with the now closed Swan Inn pub next door also playing a part. The trust intends to create an open-air cinema using the remaining wall to project films from the time, which, once a year, would include Charlie Chaplin's *The Great Dictator*.

Whilst some people feel the site should serve as a poignant reminder of WW2, others feel we should move on and it should be used for building needy residential accommodation. I believe the argument is best put by quoting the then wartime home secretary, Herbert Morrison, who said in his later autobiography: "In my experience the town that suffered most was Kingston-upon-Hull."

Also worthy of historical note is that in 1940 a short film documentary about the blitz on London was produced by the General Post Office for the Ministry of Information. Entitled *London Can Take It*, the film was widely distributed in the United States to influence America's support for Britain with the hope of them entering the war. A year later in the August of 1941 a morale boosting visit was made by King George VI and Queen Elizabeth to Hull in recognition of the city's terrible suffering (this was the same royal coupling as portrayed by Colin Firth and

74

Helena Bonham Carter in the film *The King's Speech*.) Such was the damage and devastation to Hull that a film of the royal's visit was made and a copy personally presented to President Roosevelt by the UK Ambassador to Washington. The Ambassador had also visited Hull in the September of 1941 and his brief was to persuade the Americans to enter the war, which they did in the December of 1941. To this day the film of Hull and its wartime struggle still remains in the White House Archives.

The stoicism and humour of Hull folk during the war is reflected in comments told by former Lord Mayor, Fred Beedle. As a child he found it dreadful to have to go to school the morning after an air raid and admitted: "Kids would wonder who was going to turn up and who wasn't. The only positive thing about a school pal not turning up is that you had a better chance of getting into overcrowded Saturday afternoon matinees. Though our parents were not so much bothered about cinemas getting blown-up as what they were about pubs and fish and chip shops."

The National Picture Theatre was run by the owner of the Cecil cinema located closer to Hull's city centre, which was also destroyed by bombing. In 1955, the rubble of the Cecil was finally cleared and it was totally rebuilt across the street from its original location. The brand new reconstruction of the Cecil saw it become both the city and the UK's flagship cinema. Seating 2052, it was the first new cinema to be built post-war on a new site and host to the largest Cinemascope screen in Britain. It boasted air-conditioning, a 100-seat restaurant with waitress service and a three manual Marshall Sykes theatre organ console, which rose majestically from the floor. (Less sensitive locals might have said that the Germans did us a favour for bringing such modernity to the 700-year old city of Hull.) In 1992 it became a bingo hall.

As WW2 neared its end, a terrible event took place in Hull that was thought to be an alleged war atrocity outside of the Savoy cinema (1923-1960), which was situated on Holderness Road. This road runs parallel with the Humber estuary on a horizontal east-to-west map bearing. Luftwaffe aircraft flying in from over the North Sea used Holderness Road and the Humber estuary as geographical landmarks to find Hull. The bombing targets would have mainly been the city's docks, but the falling spread of bombs was often indiscriminate. The Humber estuary landmark was also useful as a guide for enemy aircraft to fly on to further inland targets. Should the Luftwaffe's further inland missions be aborted, or they had leftover bombs, Hull was the ideal target to drop them on to lighten their load before heading back to Germany.

During bombing raids, fast and manoeuvrable fighter aircraft escorted the big lumbering high flying bombers on their missions. Fighter aircraft not on escort duty also made low flying sorties to wreak death and destruction of their own type. The targets of fighter aircraft should have been more discriminate, their targets should have been military. What happened is that innocent civilians going about their business didn't make it home on the day of the last piloted air raid of WW2.

Where the Savoy once stood, a memorial plaque on the outside wall of the new Boyes department store recalls the incident: '*Here on the site of the old Savoy cinema and in the streets nearby, when the Luftwaffe made their final attack on Hull, 17th March 1945, 12 people were killed and 22 wounded. They were the last civilian casualties of World War Two in Britain to be caused by piloted enemy aircraft. A North East Coast Town*'

I grew up nearby to where this took place. The story passed-down to me and many other Hull folk is that without warning an enemy aircraft suddenly appeared and as it dived the noise of its screaming engines were accompanied by the screams of a terrified public. Without conscience or mercy the pilot engaged his guns to cut down shoppers and Savoy cinemagoers, who were exiting an afternoon matinee. It was a turkey shoot, it was a blood bath, and it was typical from a cold hearted enemy.

However, on researching this account more thoroughly, old newspaper reports told that a low flying aircraft appeared as part of a 'tip and run raid' above the area of Holderness Road. It dropped containers of small fragmentation bombs causing many casualties and superficial damage to shops and houses. The type of explosive used was an anti personnel bomb that scatters splinters to inflict maximum casualties. The Savoy manager at the time said: "The hall was closed; therefore it was incorrect to state the bombs fell as people were leaving the cinema."

Whilst having the chance in this book to put the record straight, it gives no truth to the lie that 'all is fair in love and war'.

Before the advent of television, it was estimated that two thirds of Hull's population visited the cinema at least once a week, with some of the more affluent visiting three or four times. To understand the importance cinema played in the lives of people looking for entertainment, the Regal cinema was built in Hull in the record time of 22 weeks! Seating an impressive 2465, on its completion in January 1934 the venue was curiously billed as the first theatre in England to rely entirely on electricity for its lighting, power and heating. A brochure produced for its grand opening poetically stated: *'Electricity issues your ticket of admission. It lights the exterior of the theatre by means of high-voltage gaseous discharge neon and mercury vapour tubes and the vestibule and auditorium with cunningly-placed concealed lighting giving a soft glow calculated to enhance the beauties of the decorator's art.'* Phew! It closed in 1989.

It has to be said that some of Hull's cinemas were the type you would choose to visit only as a last resort (a well known cinema called the Marble Arch was affectionately known as the Marble Itch.) My dad told me that as a kid when in the Eureka the staff would come and spray the area with Flit Spray – and this was sometimes done while kids were sat in their seats! My dad also said that at Saturday matinees once all the kids were seated, they were kept seated. This was to stop them running riot, or running to the toilet to open windows for others to sneak in for free. This meant nobody wanted to sit in the first few front rows because that's where the urine gathered upon flowing down the sloping floor!

In other cinemas, such as the high-class sounding and ornately decorated Dorchester, you would have bragged about seeing a film there. It originally opened in 1883 as the Grand Opera House and Theatre. From its first opening until its final closure in 1979, it had several name changes and also served as a cinema and live music venue. It was as the Dorchester in April 1978 that it screened a movie with quite a buzz about it. Indeed, it is a movie that has since been credited as the single most important contribution to the history of film. A Hull cinemagoer in agreement with this – and who has the sort of name given to a secret agent – is 46-year-old, Mark Buck. As well as claiming bragging rights for being a regular of the Dorchester, back in April 1978 the then 14-year-old Mark could also claim bragging rights for having visited the cinema to see said film 54 times during its four week run. By now you may have guessed the movie was *Star Wars*. Mark's only regret is having sold an original Star Wars poster for a pittance not long after it was given to him for free by the management of the Dorchester.

However, along with keeping his 54 admission ticket stubs, he was wise enough to hang on to an original and valuable uncut Super 8mm copy of Star Wars that he acquired in 1980 for his collection as a home movie enthusiast. At 9-years-old he bought his first projector from a full year's saved-up pocket money for £20. He recalled: "It was a silent playback and so tacky the drive belt was an elastic band! It didn't actually play at the right speed either, it played too slow, but at least it made the films last longer."

Without doubt, the cinematic event for Hull in the 21st century was that the city was chosen to host the grand opening of VUE Hull in 2007, which boasts the first ever all digital multiplex in Europe (10 screens). It also boasts 'stadium seating' along with bean bags, sofa pods and sexy leather armchairs giving extra arm and leg room, a Ben and Jerry's ice cream concession, and a beer and wine dispenser. Compared to the days of yore when many venues were known as a fleapit or a bughouse, moviegoers now have little to complain about. That said, had I been one of cinema's core demographic (a teenager) my complaint would be that the leather armchairs should have been situated on the back row and not smack bang in the middle of the viewing area! As an adult my only complaint is why can't we get rum and raisin ice-cream anymore?

Another big cinematic event for Hull was that in 2010 the city was chosen to host the largest outdoor screen in Europe to show two classic films at a Drive-In. The Disney family classic *Jungle Book* and the date-movie classic *Dirty Dancing* were chosen to entice moviegoers to come and park up in Walton Street, which normally serves as a car park and event space for car boot sales and travelling fairs. A two-hundred square metre screen would be held in position by a crane and the audience could listen in by tuning their car radios to a short range FM frequency. The organiser believed in the Drive-In as a romantic idea attached to an American experience of Happy Days and the 1950's, thus the choice of the films on show. However, it seems Hull folk are not romantic enough as only 200 advance tickets were sold for the 2000 seat capacity and the show was cancelled.

Though the Drive-In experience has eluded me, in 2009 I was more than overjoyed to experience a silent movie classic starring Charlie Chaplin. (A century earlier in 1909, as part of Fred Karno's Circus, a relatively unknown Chaplin appeared in person in Hull when performing on stage at the Palace Theatre.) On becoming the most famous name in the world, in 1925 Chaplin wrote, produced, directed and starred in *The Gold Rush*. This was shown at the Albermarle Music Centre in Hull and had live accompaniment performed and composed by the Italian ensemble Gatto Marte. A house full of cineastes cheered it to the rafters. I hadn't seen the film the whole way through before, only excerpts. One of these excerpts that I'm sure you are familiar with is one of the best known scenes in film history – when Chaplin is trapped in a log cabin in the icy wastes of Alaska and he's forced to eat a leather boot to avoid starvation.

During Chaplin's early film career it is ironic that the movies were called Silents, for in the silent era nearly all films were accompanied by at least a piano if not a full-on orchestra. This particular evocation of experiencing a film as it would have been during cinema's pioneering days was simply poetry in motion pictures. But imagine being present when the Roxy movie theatre opened in New York City on 11 March 1927. At one time it employed 16 projectionists, an orchestra of 110 musicians led by four conductors, and three organists who played simultaneously on Kimball organ consoles from the orchestra pit. Known as 'The Cathedral of Motion Picture', the Roxy was once the largest cinema by seating capacity. Its original plans for an audience of 6,214 were not realised, but achieving 5920 seats was still pretty amazing! It closed in 1960.

Of the 44 pre-war cinemas in Hull, none currently operate in their original business role. The gathering interest in the National Picture Theatre is proving that it can still draw an audience. If it is saved it will be the only pre-war built cinema still operating as such in Hull and it will make the history books of having had the longest intermission in cinema history.

PICTURE PALACES

Way back in the days long before TV,

Entertainment saw kids find their own fun,

They didn't have much but come the weekend,

Full of excitement how they would all run,

Quick as the wind to their local fleapit,

To worship worthy cinematic gods,

Unlike today's youth, who luckily have,

Their fancy, hi-tech iPads and iPods.

Years later after careful restoration,

Some of those fleapits are spic-and-span clean,

Where heroes and villains of yesteryear,

Once boldly strode on their big silver screen,

When deafening roars of "hoorays!" and "boos!"

Were screamed out loud as the vocal lingo,

But where the sounds now repeatedly heard,

Are the croaking shouts of "Line" or "Bingo!"

Even more sadly not all those fleapits,

Managed to achieve a happy retirement,

Though some became pubs and others big stores,

Forlornly most were of no requirement,

And several befell a fate worse than death,

Their use became ignominiously stark,

With hurt pride many now serve the world,

As yet another ubiquitous car park!

For those cinemas in Hull that have survived as other businesses, of interest are the Regent and the Tower. They both stood on the same road directly opposite each other and were run by the same owner. Opened in 1910, the Regent closed in 1978 to become a pub, but has had the honour of seeing its old cinema frontage replicated and displayed at Hull's Streetlife Museum. Built in 1914 and closed as a cinema also in 1978, the Tower has since operated as a nightclub. (A local joke had it that when a boy was asked in school: "Where is the Bloody Tower" he answered: "Opposite the bloody Regent.")

Since becoming a nightclub, the Tower gained a notorious reputation as a seedy drinking establishment and a local euphemism for ensuring a good time was to experience 'the Tower for an hour', especially on its infamous stripper night. Though moral standards at the Tower had deteriorated, thankfully, it hadn't deteriorated as a building which is Grade II listed. In 2010 it was put up for sale at £200,000. This has seen members of the UK Cinema Theatre Association (CTA) hoping that it will find a sympathetic buyer to return it back to a picture palace. The CTA considers the Tower as being the finest untouched example of an Edwardian built cinema in England.

One of many good reasons for saving the Tower is that sitting atop of its art nouveau frontage is a stone carved female figure, allegedly based on silent era actress Mary Pickford (1892-1979). Any visit to the Tower in my days as a child always elicited a giggle for the statue is topless! Mary Pickford, who played chaste and demure characters, was billed as America's sweetheart and was never so brazen on screen – or reportedly off it, so I doubt it was created as a tribute to her. It could be said that what the figure prophetically reflected was the impiety to come during the Tower's latter days as a racy nightclub. I once visited 'the Tower for an hour' and quite honestly I enjoyed the 'live in the flesh' floorshow as an adult more than I remembered seeing the inanimate statue as a youngster!

Another reason the Tower should be saved is that prior to becoming its manager, Mr Everard Jordan was well known to the people of Hull, for it was his voice that answered when they called the 'What's On At The Hull Cinema' Phonadiary Service. More importantly, Mr Jordan organised two luncheons in honour of Laurel and Hardy during their visits to Hull when appearing live on stage at theatres in the city. Their visits to tread the boards took place in 1947 and 1953, when both luncheons were given by the Hull Society of Cinema Managers of which Everard Jordan was the chairman. Laurel and Hardy were my absolute childhood comedy heroes and how fabulous to have been present in the company of these much loved Hollywood legends, who by all accounts were as charming and funny off the screen as on it. Though there is no written record of them visiting the Tower, I think it is likely they crossed its threshold as the hotel accommodating them (The Royal Hotel) is located only yards away from the cinema. Also, Everard Jordan remained a life-long friend of Stan and Ollie after first meeting them.

One threshold they definitely – but unexpectedly – crossed was that of the Porter family. In 1947 whilst travelling to Hull from Scotland, together with their wives and agent, Laurel and Hardy were in a taxi on the road between the market town of Beverley and Hull. Just outside Beverley in the small village of Woodmansey the taxi driver pulled in for vehicle assistance at the Dixon Arms public house. One can imagine the landlord, Frederick Porter, walking back into his living room to tell his wife: "Put the kettle on darling, Laurel and Hardy have dropped by for a cup of tea!" The gobsmacked Porter family of mum, dad, three daughters and a son, provided the entourage some Yorkshire hospitality until they carried on their journey upon their taxi being fixed. Stan and Ollie returned their appreciation by sending the Porters free tickets to their show and an invite back stage. It seems that the Porter family proudly boasted about this unscripted life memory for a long time afterwards. The Dixon Arms was pulled down and replaced in 1998 by The Warton Arms. As luck would have it, I was employed in my role as a Town Crier to preside over the grand opening of The Warton Arms. It was there – fifty years on after Stan and Ollie's visit – this story was still going strong and told to me by village locals.

An acquaintance of mine told me of his unexpected delight at also seeing them. It was as a nine-year-old boy when leaving church with his mother and father after Sunday morning prayers. St Charles Borromeo Catholic Church is located opposite the New Theatre, where Laurel and Hardy were performing in 1947. His total amazement on seeing them walk by resulted in him receiving a clip-round-the-ear to calm down when he began jumping for joy and shrieking out loud with excitement. "It's Stan who was supposed to get a whack from Ollie, not me," he quipped with a smile.

He laughed when I replied: "Another fine mess someone had got themselves into."

Outside of Hollywood, I have been fortunate to have met many other big names of the silver screen right here in Hull. This opportunity comes around twice a year when as a Town Crier I herald the degree ceremonies at the University of Hull. It is when such luminaries as Dame Judi Dench, Sir Tom Courtenay, Sir Ben Kingsley, John Hurt, Omar Sharif, Michael Apted and the late Anthony Minghella, have been invited to the city to be awarded Honorary Doctorates for their contribution to the arts. Anthony Minghella, whose work included directing *The English Patient* (1996) which won nine Academy Awards, received a first class Honours degree in Drama from the university. He went on to become an inspirational lecturer in the drama department and as a tribute to his work a studio at the university has been named after him.

The University of Hull ought to invite Quentin Tarantino to receive an Honorary Doctorate. Whilst in the city the plight of both the Tower and the bombed out National Picture Theatre could be hinted at. What they need is a passionate benefactor like Tarantino who got his wish to own a movie theatre. The New Beverly, an independent cinema in Los Angeles, has an interesting past. It has been a vaudeville theatre, a night club owned by LA mob member Mickey Cohen, and a pornographic movie venue. Most significantly it was where Tarantino enjoyed watching movies in his youth. In 1978 under a new owner it began showing regular films with the draw of a double-bill, which played for nearly three decades. Then it fell on hard times and its future looked uncertain. On the quiet, Tarantino helped out with private monthly payments to keep it open. But when the New Beverly's chief operator passed away in 2007, the theatre faced closure. This prompted Tarantino to buy it outright. "I always considered the New Beverly my charity, an investment I never wanted back," he said. "As long as I'm alive and as long as I'm rich the New Beverly will be there, showing double features in 35mm."

As well as championing cinematic venues I want to briefly do the same for the much maligned projectionist. I say much maligned because the booing and hissing from audiences wasn't always aimed at a film's villain, it was aimed at the projectionist.

How many of us remember bad focusing, the sound out of sync, flickering, the burning of a cauliflower or the movie stopping altogether? As audiences voiced their displeasure, up in the projector room a frantic manager was doing the same. "What have you done?" a manager would scream at a projectionist. Swearing under his breath and with weary contempt the projectionist would calmly answer: "Do you think I did it on purpose? It's the film roll that's snapped and I will in a minute if you don't leave me to get on with fixing it!" Expert hands would then be splicing the film roll together as the manager's eyes bore a hole into the projectionist's back willing him to hurry up. For any long delays in getting the film restarted, either an apology appeared up on the screen or an embarrassed manager gave it in person. The last act in this little drama was the inevitable cheer from the audience as the film resumed and all was well with the world again, but not always so between manager and projectionist.

This is where I reintroduce Mark Buck, for he was that very same projectionist! With his passion for movies it was inevitable Mark would pursue a career in cinema. His early career saw him working as a master butcher before giving it the chop to work in retail, selling menswear. With only his 8mm home movie hobby for experience, aged 26, Mark answered an ad to be a projectionist at the UCI in Hull in 1990. Though he didn't rate his chances through his lack of big screen know-how, thankfully the interviewer recognised Mark's unbridled enthusiasm and he got the job. Two decades later, Mark could be considered one of Britain's leading projectionists.

In early cinema it took one projectionist to operate the showing of one film. In early multiplexes it took one good projectionist to operate the showing of two films at the same time. With the advent of digital cinemas many projectionists are now out of work and progressives like Mark are unfairly blamed. Mark was head-hunted to work at VUE Hull by the same cinema manager who gave him his first job. Initially the VUE was to be 35mm with 5 projectionists for its 10 screens. Instead it embraced the digital future. Employed as the sole projectionist and responsible for showing a film on each of its 10 HD screens simultaneously, these days Mark has 21st century technology at his disposal. In fully digital cinemas there is no need to handle 35mm film stock; all films arrive on computer discs.

Mark has since written the training manual on digital projection and travelled Britain teaching others the new tricks of the trade. He has mixed feelings about the passing of 35mm, the organic look and feel of film strip, the skill of manually feeding it quickly into a projector, the sound it made when whirring away and the panic to save the day, or at least to save the show when it snapped. "There'll always be a place for it as an art form in history, which is where it now belongs. I think it's only romantics that would fight its demise," he concluded.

One such romantic is electronics engineer and man of great passion for the world of cinema, David Alexander. Now 72, David has worked in many movie and legitimate theatre venues, which included the Dorchester in Hull where he was second projectionist. He is someone who clearly loves cinema in all its forms for he has a copy of every Charlie Chaplin and Buster Keaton movie, along with a mixed total of thirteen 8mm, 9.5mm, 16mm and 35mm projectors. In his home his living room resembles a movie memorabilia store and one could spend hours looking at the artefacts that fill all available space with books, photographs, pamphlets, DVDs, videos, albums, a 1/16th scale miniature Wurlitzer organ complete with a similar sized mannequin organ player, and various bits of metal and plastic that obviously have some cinematic bearing but I was too polite to ask. David is considered Hull's foremost cinema and theatre historian and as such he satisfied a curiosity of mine about why in 1955 at the grand opening of the Cecil the venue management was presented with a black cat from the guest of honour, famed British actress Dinah Sheridan. I had thought a black cat brought luck to a venue and was a superstition needed to be perpetuated, but it was simply that most cinemas of yesteryear had a cat to keep down unwanted vermin.

The Dorchester suffered more than most from vermin, namely rats, which took shelter there from the ratcatchers efforts next door at the Hull Brewery depot. If the thought of that wasn't bad enough for patrons, the thought that the Dorchester was haunted may have been worse. David had seen a ghost there several times, as had other staff members. The apparition appeared in coat-tails, carrying a violin and sporting the distinguishing feature of long grey hair. David researched who it might be and discovered that when the Dorchester was the Grand Theatre venue a member of the orchestra had committed suicide by hanging himself in a dressing room.

It was on Friday and Monday mornings when all new films were privately viewed by projectionists to check their quality for exhibition and timing. The Dorchester's cat that followed David everywhere loved to be present during these checks but only on a Monday morning, never on a Friday. In one instance the cat was found and physically held in place on a Friday morning check but ran off after a fight to escape. Friday was the day of the week when the ghost, nicknamed Charlie, always appeared and it was on a Friday that Charlie had killed himself!

Special screenings at the Dorchester saw David enjoying the challenge of adding a touch of showmanship. In doing so, what follows is a story he nostalgically regaled, which by today's sophisticated standards may seem somewhat tame – kitsch even – but nonetheless good theatrical fun.

Prior to the start at the Northern premiere of *Dracula* (1958) starring Christopher Lee, all of the house lights were switched off and for what seemed an eternity an uneasy silence befell the auditorium. The venue's organ (which had been covered in black-out material and could not be seen) rose up through its usual trap door entrance. Placed on top of it with its lid half open was a white painted coffin (borrowed from the local Co-op undertakers). The intention to spook the audience was heightened as David shone a slit-green spotlight directly on to the coffin. Of course, this eerie scene would have been made even creepier had the ghost of Charlie climbed out of the coffin! What happened next though was just as dramatic... The recording of a female scream played at full volume suddenly tore through the air. This had audience members leaping out of their seats and several screaming in return. A deep baritone voice then uttered the words: "The ghosts are restless tonight." This was followed by a recording of horrible laughter. The film then finally began for the enjoyment of those less nervous types who hadn't run out of the cinema. It was only at each last showing of the evening when this stunt took place and when, prudently, St John's Ambulance services were invited to attend.

HOW TO GET INTO THE MOVIES!

For those whose love is movie going,

And are looking for ways to fund it,

Why bother paying as a mere punter,

Instead be a sponging movie pundit!

But if aloof critics make you despair,

And plainly you've more integrity,

Then be an actor and you might appear,

On silver screens everywhere for free,

Or you could reach for even more still,

Aim for where the almighty sits,

The exalted seat that's up in the gods,

Yes, the one of the projectionist.

I hope that those of you reading this book who are not from Hull have found it to be of general interest and fun. I also hope those of you from Hull feel the same and that you are not too disappointed if I haven't written about your favourite cinema. It was not my intention to cover all of the 44 venues that once existed in the city; however, there are just three more that I would like to mention beginning with the Langham. This cinema boasted the largest seating capacity in the city, 2800. Without exaggeration its foyer was the length of a bowling alley and it was said that several double-decker buses could have parked up in this space. Situated on Hessle Road it served the 'Wild West' hard-working and hard-case community of Hull's fishing industry. (Hull was once the greatest deep-sea trawling port in the world and fishing served as the city's industrial livelihood, which has since been reduced from nearly 400 trawlers to a pathetic and scandalous nothing!) Hessle Road had the largest concentration of people in the city and during the fishing heydays the place was a magnet for entertainment much more wildly lived than anything that ever appeared on cinema screens. In between trips to sea, though the trawler lad's boozing money may have soon run out, there were always a few shillings leftover to buy tickets for nursing a hangover while watching a film at the Langham. The choice of film would have mostly been a Western, which reflected the trawler lads' lifestyles!

The Langam was also where Sir Tom Courtenay – Hull's most well known cinema related celebrity – spent his movie going youth and, I would guess, dreamed of one day achieving silver screen success.

The penultimate cinema I want to mention is the Astoria on Holderness Road. This is where back in the late fifties a talented musician jammed with his band on the stage. John Barry was the musician's name and he was born in nearby York, where his father, Jack Xavier Prendergast (who was a projectionist in the silent movie era), owned several movie theatres in the north of England, the Astoria in Hull being one them. Often while watching a film, Barry would note with pen and paper what worked or what didn't. Although not strictly a son of Hull, nonetheless the city would like to claim him for he cut his musical teeth on the stage of the Astoria. He changed his name from Prendergast to Barry and with his band, The John Barry Seven, he performed rock 'n' roll numbers on Sunday evenings when his instrument of choice was the trumpet.

Inspired in his youth by days spent in the cinema it rewarded him most handsomely in later life, for he won five film score Oscars, including countless other musical awards. As well as composing Bond scores such as *Goldfinger* (1964) and *You Only Live Twice* (1967), he wrote the soundtrack for *Born Free* (1966), *Out Of Africa* (1985) and *Dancing With Wolves* (1991). My own favourite piece of his work is the instrumental music for *Midnight Cowboy* (1969). The Hull Daily Mail paid a tribute to him on his untimely death from a heart attack aged-77 in January 2011.

The ultimate cinema I want to mention (that's ultimate as in final but not as in fabulous) is the Royalty. As a kid I absolutely loved the stylish sounding names of all the movie theatres in and around Hull. I was especially fond of those beginning with an 'R', such as the Rex, Rialto, Regent, Ritz and Regal, but none of those could beat the Royalty, which served the residents on the kitchen-sink estate where I grew up. Although it boasted a splendidly posh name it must be said that the good folk who patronised the Royalty were anything but!

Everyone has their own special movie memories and I would argue that it is most profound when we are kids. It's when we can eat cinema treats without worrying about calories, cholesterol and – because our parents are usually paying – their cost. Also it's when we believe in whatever foolishness is happening on the big screen and we don't feel foolish for believing it.

My love for the movies was formed along with all the other kids in my native Yorkshire, who grew up in the late 50's and early 60's. That's when the Saturday matinee ruled at the cinema and when in 1963, as a restless eleven-year-old lad, I witnessed one of the best fantasy films to ever do the rounds. I saw *Jason And The Argonauts* back-to-back and would have watched it for a third time but the ushers turfed me out. I had to get back for my tea anyway. Running like the wind I arrived home and breathlessly pleaded with my mother to advance me my next week's pocket money. I wanted to catch the film once more at the early evening show. With promises of not sulking I offered to wash the pots, make the beds, pick up litter in the garden and do the shopping. I even promised to stop stealing the milk off the next door neighbours' doorstep. ANYTHING! My mother calmed me down and administered the brown paper bag technique for preventing asthmatic attacks. Then tightly clutching several of her hard-earned pennies I was sent on my way.

Sporting a grin wider than any silver screen in Britain and ignoring my mum's plea not to run I arrived back at the Royalty in good time. In my chewing-gum-stained seat I devoured every frame of the fantasy adventures of the heroic Jason, which was the day that had me forever hooked on the movies.

It wasn't a wealthy family that I grew up in and buying comics like the weekly Beano or Dandy was not routine. When my mother took us into Hull city centre, I used to pester her to walk by the many cinemas located there so that I could look at the movie posters, which for me was the next best thing to reading a weekly comic. That's how hooked I was on the movies.

The Royalty closed down in 1966 and became a supermarket. The saving grace for that year was the television, which brought on the downfall of cinema's dominance in the first place! For the whole summer of '66 we thankfully had the football World Cup to watch. This was when England beat Germany 4-2 in the final, in what was considered by many jingoistic Brits as better than any war film in which we also beat the Germans.

Before television I think that schools existed to ensure mothers didn't go mad and cinemas existed to ensure kids didn't go mad when school was closed. When television came along I also think the behaviour of kids improved. Defying authority at a picture house when being rowdy and throwing popcorn was one thing, but daring to defy authority at home... My stern mother would never have stood for the same grief we often dished out to any introvert cinema ushers. On reflection I don't recall that in the Royalty kids ever had popcorn fights, real fights yes! There weren't that many kids with the money to buy such a treat and it was far too yummy to waste anyway. Throwing popcorn was also seen as a bit of girly thing to do, especially when in its place most kids scooped-up loose gravel from a nearby garage forecourt to use as proper ammunition. Combined with an ice-lolly stick as a launch pad, flicking gravel could often be more fun than watching some of the corny old serials featured on the screen.

When not at the cinema and watching television at home any missiles that might have been thrown were usually by my volatile mother at my long suffering father. My childhood television viewing habits were dictated by my mother's tastes; she unquestionably ruled the roost and the choice of all television programs. The films I had to watch had fast-talking Cary Grant and Katherine Hepburn in screwball comedies, or, if lucky, slow-talking Gary Cooper in westerns. A regular Sunday afternoon routine was the chore of sitting through a musical. Sorry, but it was action films for me and the stars I mostly fell in love with were Errol Flynn, Burt Lancaster and big John Wayne. If pressed to name my overall favourite I would say that England has St George and America has always had John Wayne.

One film my mother always loved to watch was *Doctor Zhivago* (1965). On the film's release my mother insisted we see it as a family at the pictures. This wasn't because it featured Hull born Tom Courtenay; it was because it featured the romantic lead of Egyptian born Omar Sharif. It also had the haunting sound track of

Lara's Theme. Whenever I hear it I am immediately transported back in time to a flip-up seat in the Royalty, where I am using a little wooden spoon to scrape every last morsel from a tub of rum and raisin ice-cream before licking the tub clean and trying not to let my mother see my bad manners, though back in those days this would have been difficult through the haze of cigarette smoke that permeated auditoriums to which my chain-smoking mother contributed.

When video machines became the rage I dared to buy one for my mother. Accompanied by a haze of cigarette smoke, though this time contributed by me as I tried to stay calm when trying to explain the video instructions to my baffled mother, the first film she finally managed to play on it was *Doctor Zhivago*. But after my mother had passed away how cheerless I felt when through my work as a Town Crier I couldn't tell her of my joy at meeting Tom Courtenay and Omar Sharif. A further disappointment is not having met Julie Christie (yet), who was the one person in the film that I always had my eyes on.

On the actress front, in my early youth I will admit to having had a crush on Judy Garland in *The Wizard Of Oz* and Elizabeth Taylor in *National Velvet*. But reaching my teens these two were soon dumped upon seeing Ann-Margret in *Viva Las Vegas* and Raquel Welch in *One Million Years BC*. My teenage hormones were then telling me not to commit my confused but pure little heart to any specific screen-siren after seeing Jane Fonda in *Barbarella*.

As a youngster, going to the pictures was where I could live beyond my dreams but sadly not beyond my means. However, odd jobbing earned me extra pocket moncy to allow me to see my own choice of films rather than those my mother wanted to watch. Nothing could beat seeing for the first time *The Magnificent Seven* (1960), *Zulu* (1964), *The Dirty Dozen* (1967) and the James Bond movies. This was a time when Sean Connery was the only decent 007, who all young lads wanted to be. Also at the time, a counterpoint to James Bond were family oriented Disney films of which I'll admit that the musical *Mary Poppins* was a revelation. But Julie Andrews was no competition for the Bond girls, who all young lads wanted to be with!

On reaching my autumn years, my love for watching movies (and Bond girls) is as strong as ever, but not at home. Where else other than the cinema do you get to see the 'coming soon' trailers, voiced-over by a fellow with tones like a chainsaw cutting through concrete, in Dolby Surround Sound and with the volume switched up to eleven? Where else can you people-watch in supersize and everyone is beautiful except the villains, who usually get bumped off anyway? Where else can you enjoy a movie before it's released on DVD or appears on TV and not already know the ending? Where else can you spend the best two-hours-time-out-of-life enjoying the on screen chemistry of the hero and heroine and the off screen chemistry of an oversized bucket of popcorn washed down by a gallon of fizzy drink? Where else is there a better babysitter for children, a better meeting place for teenagers to fumble their way through adolescence, or a better way for adults to fondly remember carefree days of their youth? And as everyone from a film-star-wannabe sat in a flip-up seat, through to the most rich and famous of Hollywood players sat in a stretch-limo will concur, where else indeed!

PART THREE

A PERFECT TEN (AND A NOT SO PERFECT TEN)

**Movie nuts and non movie nuts
are people who feel sorry for each other.**

A PERFECT TEN

A projector beams a one-dimensional luminous light

onto a screen that gives birth to two dimensional life

as a voyeuristic three-dimensional audience

whilst cocooned in a four walled auditorium

sit in anticipation of five star entertainment.

Enter a squared-jawed hero boasting a six pack

and a heroine cast from seventh heaven

in the eighth instalment of a money making franchise

which has studio chiefs dancing on cloud nine

because ten out of ten critics hailed it the year's best film!

The above title would seem appropriate if awarding top marks for a perfect cinema experience. But what would be awarded to me for the list that follows in which I declare my top ten movies is a different matter! Though *Pirates Of The Caribbean* is not one of them, Johnny Depp earned my award of Poetry In Motion Pictures for the Best Movie Entrance, when, in the first film of the series, his character of Jack Sparrow is revealed and then shortly afterwards he steps off his sinking ship onto a port's boardwalk.

What Tom Mix did for a packed cinema of excited young kids in Hull, back in 1938, Johnny Depp as Jack Sparrow also did in 2010 for a class full of gobsmacked school kids at St Meridian Primary School, in Greenwich, London, where he made another unforgettable entrance. The Disney film company were filming the fourth in the series of Pirates of The Caribbean near to the school. A speculative request written to the company by one of its schoolgirls, 9-year-old, Beatrice Delap, read: "We are a bunch of pirates. Normally we're a right handful, but we're having trouble mutinying against the teachers. We'd love it if you could come and help."

To which Jack Sparrow did by bounding in to tell the class: "Maybe we shouldn't mutiny today because there are police outside monitoring me." Priceless!

Unlike Jack Sparrow, whose usual behaviour sees him failing to nail his colours to anyone's mast, I'm prepared to nail to the mast of historic record a list of my ten favourite movies. This may have you smiling with fond affection, or determined to start a hate website and see me walking the plank. My list is based on the impact each movie had on first seeing them and how they still continue to entertain. (Note that they are listed chronologically rather than in any pecking order.)

Singing In The Rain (1952). Whilst I am not a big fan of film-musicals this was the exception. Its exuberant, Technicolor, song and dance lustre just leaps off the screen to grab you by the hand and have you dancing in your seat. Why this wins out over other any other musical is that it has a half decent storyline, its titular song still resonates today and above all it was genuinely funny, which many musicals are painfully not.

Jason And The Argonauts (1964). This is the one that made me a lifelong fan of Ray Harryhausen's fantastic stop-motion animation work. Watching it along with hundreds of other kids we knew that Jason didn't need to waste time trying to stab bony skeletons with swords and collectively we shouted: "Chop their heads off... chop their bloody heads off!" (I last shouted this in 2010 at those responsible for bringing the remake of Ray Harryhausen's classic *Clash Of The Titans* to the screen. It confirmed that no special effect is beyond CGI, which can give a movie jaw dropping trickery, but it cannot give it a heart and soul.)

The Graduate (1967). I considered it training for teenagers like me growing-up at the time, who mostly saw it underage which, of course, added further excitement. If movies had to feature musical songs then this movie's soundtrack showed how to do it. Though I now use an iPod, I still have the original dog-eared album-cover and much scratched vinyl that the movie spurred me to go out and buy.

Easy Rider (1969). Aged sixteen I was getting too old for John Wayne. Peter Fonda, Denis Hopper and Jack Nicholson were the new Hollywood cowboys that I wanted to be – and still do!

THE HOPPER ON THE CHOPPER

Once a drug-popper riding a chopper

Was the out of control, Dennis Hopper,

Never reliant and never compliant

and right till the end... ever defiant,

This hell-raising chancer had no answer

to survive the fate of prostate cancer,

He often reviled, he often beguiled

and his headstone should read: BORN TO BE WILD.

Again this was a movie with a belter of a soundtrack, which I added to my growing collection of albums along with music from the movie *Woodstock* (1970). Seeing *Easy Rider* had a profound effect on me; it made me determined to get away from home as fast I could to see something of the world. Not having control of the television at home was bad enough, but as a teenager not having control of the family record player either...

The tag line from *Easy Rider* was: "A man went looking for America and couldn't find it anywhere." I thought this a strange thing to say and I hoped to one day visit America to prove it untrue, which I did and it was. Before finally making it over there I pretty much managed to visit the rest of the world courtesy of the army in which I served for 22-years. How ironic, though, that a movie about drug taking, law breaking and long haired hippies could inspire me to seek a life of adventure as a short haired, drug free, conscientious career soldier. But back in the early 1970's there weren't that many alternatives to avoiding a life on a factory production-line without committing to organisations like the military, which at least fulfilled its promise of travel abroad.

In my youth what hooked me the most about the movies was not so much an interest to be someone else (i.e. the square-jawed movie hero); it was more of a need to be *somewhere* else, especially every time I saw exotic foreign locations up there on the big widescreen. I can only but thank the movies for giving me wanderlust and the dream of one day riding across the states on a Harley.

Butch Cassidy And The Sundance Kid (1969). A western released in the same year as Sam Peckinpah's majestically violent *The Wild Bunch*, but which didn't need to rely on the spilling of claret or well trodden cowboy cliché. Instead, it had watchable laid-back leads on the top of their game (this included Katherine Ross as much as Paul Newman and Robert Redford) all delivering believable dialogue in a cracking story. And with William Goldman as its scriptwriter, well, they don't come much better than him. Loosely based on real events it has the best ever freeze-frame movie ending. The film's quality is reflected by its 4-Oscar and 9-Bafta awards, which is more Baftas than any other movie to date.

***Thunderbolt And Lightfoot* (1975).** This has the same qualities for Butch and Sundance, but set in modern times. Jeff Bridges has since been one of my favourite actors, especially after stealing the movie from right under the nose of the ever watchable Clint Eastwood.

***The Man Who Would Be King* (1975).** When forgotten classics are talked about this is up there with the best. The plot has two British soldiers in India deciding to resign from the Army and set themselves up as deities in Kafiristan - a land where no white man has set foot since Alexander. Two of Britain's best loved actors, Sean Connery and Michael Caine, took on the roles that Director John Huston had wanted Clarke Gable and Humphrey Bogart respectively to fill. It contains the lesser quoted memorable movie line by Connery as Billy Fish, who asks Caine as Peachy Carehan: "He wants to know if you are gods?" Peachy replies: "Not gods - Englishmen. The next best thing!" Of course Connery and Caine know how to deliver a line, e.g., "Yesh, mish Moneypenny," and "My name is Michael Caine," which Caine never uttered, until given the line to use as an in-joke in *Educating Rita* (1983).

***Local Hero* (1984).** I like how everything in America is big and clever. I like how they like Brits and think we are so smart. I like how this film proves it without being smug. I like how it has no car chases or explosions and the English leads don't have perfect teeth.

***Cinema Paradiso* (1990).** A beautifully crafted movie that shows it's not just output from Oscar and Bafta English speaking film industries that matter. Its portrayal of the passage of time had me nostalgic for my youth and wishing that that a kid's volunteer scheme had been in place at my local cinema. This is *the* movie to watch about movie going.

***Avatar* (2009).** Three hours worth of movie, in 3-D, and a free invite to its premiere – what's not to like? That said I have paid to see it twice more since; once with the missus who is not a fan of cinema but enjoyed this experience, and once with my son (aged 12) who said it beat *Iron Man* as the best film he had ever seen. Though this good old fashioned western in space had dodgy dialogue and an iffy plot, if you think it's easy to put a spectacle like this together and pull it off then go ahead and do it. There are some that knock Jim Cameron's means to an end, but if the end result is profit would you put your money on him or on the British team who, in the entire history of motion pictures, gave us the worst film ever made: *The Sex Lives Of Potato Men* (2004).

GUILTY PLEASURE

***Battlefield Earth* (2000).** Some films that fall into the category of worst film ever made can, in their own special way, also be a classic. As a fan of sci-fi I am more than happy at adding this to my list, albeit as an add-on guilty pleasure. For those readers asking themselves what can I be thinking... you firstly need to ask John Travolta just what the hell *he* was thinking? In my defence I would say some films are worth watching as they are a challenge for the audience to figure them out; and they don't come more challenging than this. But most importantly it needs to be seen for the following three reasons: 1) Can there be a better argument for not bringing back platform shoes and flared trousers, 2) None of us should ever again complain about having a bad hair day, 3) On the days that you think to yourself can things in life ever get worse, this is always a hoot to watch and realise that yes they can, but you're not to blame.

EPILOGUE

Had I ended this book on my top ten movies and left you with the last paragraph discussing the merits of *Battlefield Earth*, I realise it could have caused some of you to hurl my book across the floor. (When it comes to hurling, this is something you might have already done on your first viewing of John Travolta's folly.) For those who don't agree that it falls into the 'it's so bad it's good' category I hope to make amends by finishing on William Shakespeare.

In the early days of cinema, American film producers thought they needed to broaden its appeal beyond the working classes. The themes of films shifted from the prosaic of everyday life to films featuring classic Shakespeare plays. Whilst this action may have attracted a so called art elite it also helped that these plays had public domain status which avoided copyright issues. As such there are over 400 films of Shakespeare's plays in many languages making him the most filmed author.

Almost certainly the silver screen's greatest populariser of Shakespeare was the classical actor Laurence Olivier, with his magnum opus being *Henry V* (1943), which earned him a Best Actor Oscar. Other recent films of note have been Baz Lurmann's hip and energetic musical *Romeo and Juliet* (1996), and also the Shakespeare inspired *Shakespeare In Love* (1998) that deservedly earned the prize of Best Picture Oscar.

My favourite passage from the Bard's work comes from the play As You Like It, in which the melancholy character of Jacques, in Act II, Scene 7, compares life to a play and he catalogues the seven ages of man's life.

Four centuries later, inspired by Shakespeare, I leave you with my modest attempt at comparing life to a movie, catalogued in seven ages and applicable to both man and woman. If one can imagine my final poetic

offering being performed in the voice of a modern day Jack,
such as Jack Nicholson, hopefully it might chime with you
in three ways: as a reader, as a filmgoer and as an admirer
of Shakespeare.

THE SEVEN ACT MOVIE OF LIFE

The world is just one epic movie
in which we make intros and outros,
When men and women play many parts
in life's seven ageing scenarios.

First it's the look-at-me wailing call
from ten tiny fingers and ten tiny toes,
As cameras record our giggles and tears
nappies soon become forgotten curios.

Next comes a schoolchild imagination
on which boundaries no one can impose,
In mud we traipse and in puddles we splash
and the world's a popcorn smell to our nose.

A big change then brings on a rebellion
against that causing us teenage woes,
Whilst meantime we play lovers dressed-to-kill
looking to woo all would be beaus.

On becoming an adult, professions beckon
and whether arts or sciences are chose,

That perfect take will always be sought
be it with dagger and pantyhose,
Or technical eyes looking through a lens
trying to capture life's joys or sorrows.

Reward can follow and the moment is seized
as sex, drugs and rock 'n' roll flows,
Life is sweet and success should last
but, lo, it's only the Emperor's new clothes,
Since neither wealth, nor power, nor fame
can, without end, in time be froze.

The sixth age sees some hiding the cracks
to try and avoid unwelcome elbows,
As age and girth grow, looks and wits wane
and the doors of opportunity close,
Then nearing the end of our lifelong movie
we hang up either our gowns or tuxedos.

The last scene of all is when on the screen
the words of **The End** finally shows,
The audience departs, but we can't move
as the curtains slowly draw to a close,
We look around and we're all alone
in the quiet of empty silent rows
All is so cold and all is so still...
sans light, sans dark, sans shadows.

Coming soon

GO AHEAD HOLLYWOOD,
MAKE MY DAY!

...and this time it's personal